THE GOLDEN PLECTRUM

STUDIES IN CLASSICAL ANTIQUITY - Band 4

Rodopi

AMSTERDAM 1982

THE
GOLDEN PLECTRUM

Sexual Symbolism in Horace's *Odes*

by
Richard Minadeo

© Editions Rodopi B.V., Amsterdam 1982
Printed in the Netherlands
ISBN: 90—6203--664—3

for

Maria and Daniel

TABLE OF CONTENTS

PREFACE

For studies in the Classics that take radically
new directions, the support of respected seniors, more
than welcome, is vital if a dispassionate audience is
to be assured. I am therefore especially grateful to
Professors J. P. Elder and Frank O. Copley, through
whose endorsement this work has reached publication.
I extend deep thanks as well to Professors Ernest
Fredricksmeyer and Ernest Ament, both for their en-
couragement and for the close reading to which they
subjected the fair copy, and to my chief collaborators,
the many students with whom most of the ideas herein
were tested and refined. Finally, to the editors of
Latomus and The Classical Journal my thanks for per-
mission to reprint certain portions of the present
work.

Except for 3:28, 15f., where I follow Bennett,
the Latin text is Wickham's.

CHAPTER ONE
BACKGROUND AND METHOD

Till recent times the Horace of the _Odes_ has been
appreciated preeminently as a master of surfaces. He
charms the ear, dazzles the eye and, all in all, sets
common good sense to an unforgettable music. These
praises came, as they must, at a substantial price. He
shows no great gifts of intellect, emotion or imagination. In particular, he has nothing new, not even anything really important to say. His virtue is that what
he chose to say was never said so well.

The fact is that the lyrics do not display nearly
the surface clarity and finish that this body of opinion
implies. Consider, for instance, the opaqueness of the
Soracte ode, of either Vergil ode, of the Lalage and
Europa odes, indeed, of the "Ship of State" and Bandusia
odes, not to mention that most baffling conundrum of
them all, the Archytas ode. Add the obscurity posed by
numerous individual figures and passages and the very
poet whose critical writings urge a painstaking refinement may seem to have reserved a second, less exacting
standard for his own creations.

More important, the lyrics are not so superficial
as the older criticism liked to maintain. Latter day
critics, notably Poschl, Fraenkel and Commager, have be-

gun to disclose a sinuous and sturdy intellect, an ample
imagination and even an authentic emotional power behind
the _Odes_. Still, the very fact that the obscurities
just noted continue to lack explanations suggests that
much remains to be discovered before we come to grips
with Horace on his own terms.

The deficiency is owed to a poverty of method. The
clearest advances in the criticism of the _Odes_ concern
principles of design. We have learned that the matter
of placement, whether of an individual sound or of entire odes, is always worth our exquisite care. Similarly, we are trained to count lines and stanzas, to look
to the center, to seek out sectional correspondences and
the like, all for sufficient reasons. Otherwise, however, Horatian criticism has amounted largely to an extension of scholarly commentary fortified by a fluid
impressionism. Methods of critical approach developed
in this century have meanwhile all but lain unexplored.
The result is that, though we have learned more than is
entirely useful about such questions as Horace's Greek
models, the matter of his imagistic technique, which is
to say the heart of his lyric expressionism, still
awaits disciplined analysis. I quote from Owen Lee, who
provides the latest word on Horace's symbolism, to demonstrate the liklihood:[1]

> The great symbols of existence are as
> much in evidence in Horace's _Odes_ as
> they are in Mallarmé. Wind and water,
> fire and flowers, wine and gods recur in
> almost predictable patterns, not because
> Horace always intends it so, but simply
> because he thinks imaginatively. These
> images are seldom, if ever, symbols with

2

> separate meanings. The reader is not
> tempted to attach a fixed significance
> to them as he finds them again and
> again in the poems.

The one hope of verifying such a proposition would lie
in testing such images against every recognized symbolic
system. Far from supplying anything of the sort, Lee is
at pains to demonstrate in the imagery precisely that
shallow splendor which the older critics mistook in the
lyrics at large.

The present study will combine three pathways of
critical approach, one of them well-established in previous Horatian criticism, one well known but haphazardly
explored and a third that is entirely new. The novelty,
of course, will be the approach through sexual symbolism. If this is doomed to appear outlandish to some,
the remaining two are conservatism itself. We will keep
an interested eye on the order of arrangement among the
lyrics, and we will pay scrupulous attention to the com-
binational potential of detail. If these last seem too
trivial or routine to require formulation, let me try
to suggest how urgently they apply to the unending task
of elucidating the Odes. We shall find that, even in
so obviously a patterned ensemble as the Roman odes,
neither the overall structure nor the concert of individual details has been as yet adequately disclosed. Likewise, as massive an alteration in arrangement as results
from Horace's addition of a fourth book to the original
ensemble, it has gone amazingly uncatalogued, whether in
the changes of structure, attitude or emotional coloring
entailed.[2]

As for the symbolism, we shall presently see that,

3

foreign though it may be to Horatian criticism, it traces back in the poetic tradition all the way to Homer.
Moreover, it is evident that, like Horace himself, his
predecessors employed it with as much calculation as
they might any other figurative effect. As it happens,
the case for deliberateness is most readily substantia-
ted in the Odes, but the contextual aptness of the
specimens to follow will convince the fair-minded that
Homer, Euripides, Aristophanes, Catullus and Vergil,
these at least, employed the device with conscious purpose.

First, however, let us survey the symbolic forms
which Horace favored. Highest on the list are the
images of the tree and of water. The first represents
the phallus, the second, on a general plane, the female
principle and, at its most specific, the vagina. Both
figures, of course, will have their analogues and
variants. The weapon, the ship, the snake, the bird,
the thunderbolt, the wand, plectrum and thyrsus will all
intimate the male, while images of wine and earth, together with the concavity, receptacle, entryway and en-
closure will suggest the female. Thus, the house and
its humble counterpart, the cave, figure among the
poet's favorite female sexual emblems. As a corollary,
any female symbol save the sea may signify the womb.
Likewise, the phallus, especially as symbolized by the
tree, will often be invoked for its progenitive and not
merely its erotic associations. One major symbol remains. Horace frequently employs wind imagery to signify the passions, sexual passion in particular. The
following tabulation will indicate that, in principle,
this congeries of symbolic values came as his poetic

inheritance.

Just before his long and enervating detention by
the nymphomaniacal Calypso, Odysseus barely escapes
drowning in Charybdis by grasping hold of an enormous
fig tree rooted in the adjacent cliffs (Od. 12:431ff.)
and clinging thereto "like a bat." Why a tree? Why,
specifically, a fig tree? Only symbolism can explain,
and the symbolism is lucid. The fig tree, besides
phallic, is fruitful. It attaches to life and, more
vitally, to provision for life. Far from an arbitrary
convenience of plot, then, this enormous tree of life
to which the hero clings represents, through intimations
of strength and fruitfulness, the very physical and
moral aretē clinging to which he not merely survives but
restores himself as lord and husband, father and provi-
der in his own house. Nor is this all. It clarifies
itself further by anticipating a cognate symbol later
on--the olive tree from which Odysseus' connubial bed
was carved and around which his bedchamber and, hence,
his entire palace and domestic life was constructed.
If much more than simple phallicism emerges from all
of this, it merely shows the expressive wealth of the
symbolism. As for the whirlpool, this through its vaginal suggestion obviously signifies Calypso's sexual
voracity. In social terms it represents the death from
which the life-signifying tree is deliverance and
restoration.[3]

The symbols of water and tree also keenly illumi-
nate Phaedra's ravings at the beginning of the Hippolytus. Addressing her uncomprehending old nurse, the
lovestruck queen exclaims (208ff.):

Oh, that I might draw a draught of

> pure water from a dewy fountlet and,
> lying in a grassy meadow beneath the
> poplars, find respite.

The nurse presently responds (225ff.):

> Why do you yearn for flowing springs?
> Close by the towers is a watered slope
> whence to draw your draughts.

Justin Glenn has taken up the sexual symbolism of
Phaedra's utterance both here and elsewhere in the
scene with, all in all, brilliant results.[4] Throughout
on the primary level the imagery suggests only that
Phaedra wants to join Hippolytus in his habitual haunts
and activities. But, symbolically, as Glenn shows, her
fierce desire for Hippolytus himself shines through:
the poplars suggest the phallus, her reclining position
beneath them suggests what it suggests, and the deep
(literally, "long-haired") grasses imply the vagina.
Her wish a moment later (219f.) to wield a pointed
javelin is, as Glenn observes, also transparently sexual.

Where our particular passage is concerned, however,
Glenn attempts to impress phallic imagery upon the foun-
tain imagery, and here, if nothing else, the nurse's
response rules him out of order. The towers, like the
poplars in Phaedra's ravings, clearly indicate the
phallus, while the "watered slope," corresponding to
the earlier "dewy fountlet," carries an equally transparent feminine suggestion. Phaedra's desire to drink
of the pure, remote fount would thus add up to a wish-
fulfilling fantasy par excellence: she wants the benefit of her own nature (the water itself) both out of

6

wedlock (the remoteness of the scene) and outside of
guilt (the stress on purity). The nurse's answer is
thus also turned neatly to account, positing civilized
and proper sexual gratification in place of the illicit
and wild.

The same sexual imagery contributes handsomely to
the parodos of the <u>Lysistrata</u> (254-387). Here Jeffrey
Henderson's trailblazing study shows the way. The chief
value for us in Henderson's work lies in the lengthy
lists he provides of the symbolic terms which Aristophanes employs for the sexual parts--a tabulation, obviously, which may be cited in evidence for Horace's
own usage.[5]

Henderson briefly touches upon the parodos, men-
tioning the phallic "flaming rams" with which the chorus
of old men intend to rout the barricaded women[6] and
stressing that the battle between these old worthies and
their female compeers "is meant to symbolize the violent
quality of male phallic thrusting versus the woman's
rooted steadfastness."[7] This, though accurate enough
as far as it goes, omits most of the symbolic fun.
First, it is clear that the old men intend to burn rather than batter their way to victory. Throughout, meanwhile, they groan under the weight of the huge logs they
heft and have a terrible time nursing the flame in the
firepots they carry. Their implied sexual ambition--
enormous, given their years--is duly reduced to nothing.
Old women appear armed only with pitchers of water, and,
after a verbal skirmish which they clearly win, they
extinguish the old men's ardors by means of a single,
swift dousing. The symbolic scherzo persists right to
the close:

    W. Ch. What? Wasn't it warm?
    M. Ch. Warm? Stop it! What are you doing?
    W. Ch. I'm watering you, so that you'll sprout.
    M. Ch. But I'm already withered from shivering.
    W. Ch. Well, since you've brought fire, warm
            yourself at it.

On the Roman side, Catullus displays an obvious familiarity with sexual symbolism in his description of the inert husband of a beautiful young bride (C. 17, 10ff.):

> . . . ludere hanc sinit ut libet, nec pili facit uni,
> nec se sublevat ex sua parte, sed velut alnus
> in fossa Liguri iacet suppernata securi,
> tantundem omnia sentiens quam si nulla sit usquam,
> talis meus stupor nil videt, nihil audit,
> ipse qui sit utrum sit aut non sit, id quoque nescit.

> . . . he lets her frolic as she likes and neither gives a damn nor, on his own part, rouses himself at all, but, just as an alder hamstrung by a Ligurian axe lies in a ditch with no more awareness than nullity itself, so my good dullard sees nothing, hears nothing and knows not who he is nor even if he is or is not.

There is an inescapable symbolism not only in the figures of tree and ditch, but in sublevat and parte as well.

    The same tree figures oppositely in Vergil's declaration at the close of the Eclogues that his love for Gallus "will grow as much hour by hour as the green alder shoots up when the Spring is young." Vergil also treats us to a stunning piece of vaginal imagery when Aeneas first arrives at the Libyan shore (Aen. 1:157ff.). The Trojans sail into a deep (longo recessu), placid inlet sheltered on either side by lofty cliffs. So far,

a palpable intimation of the welcoming female, but there
is more. At the head of the inlet the cliffs are darkly
wooded and house beneath their brow a watered cave. The
cave prefigures not only the place in which Aeneas and
Dido will consummate their passion, but, surely, the
intimate Dido herself.

We will close this little survey with an offering
from the earlier writings of our own poet. Stopping
off in Apulia on the way to Brundisium, Horace and his
party are put up for a night at a farm cottage. Seemingly in passing, the poet mentions that the burning of
wet boughs, leaves and all, in the fireplace brought
tears to the eyes (Sat. 5:80f.). But then he tells how
a failed assignation with a local girl cost him a bout
of erotic dreams and a discommoding nocturnal emission:
the bother of incomplete combustion all over again.

What significance has such symbolism for Horace's
lyrics? Let us start with some bold particulars. For
some few crucial pieces, odes whose very coherence has,
admittedly or not, eluded comprehension for centuries,
it reveals the very essence. By contrast, it will
occasionally belie an interpretation that time and com-
placency have rendered sacrosanct. More often, no such
misapprehension is involved, and we simply find contexts, on their literal faces suggesting nothing of love,
transformed by the symbolism into erotic statements of
considerable variety and point.

Less enterprisingly, as in the amatory odes proper,
the symbolism will often merely elaborate upon the main
theme. At the same time, its work is scarcely restricted
to erotic expression alone. Just as the ultimate function of sexuality in nature is procreation, so in Horace

do its emblems range beyond the adumbration of sexual
weal and woe to a variegated exploration of the creative impulse. Hence we shall find that the impulse behind Rome's political vitality, the combination of
virtus and consilium which, in the poet's eyes, first
empowered and might, with luck, preserve her dominion,
is brought home most forcefully by nothing other than
the impress of sexual symbolism. Likewise, and no less
crucially, the considerable body of lyrics that centers
on the power of music finds its richest expression in
the resources of the symbolic technique.

Having mentioned love, politics and the muse, we
touch upon all of the poet's major preoccupations save,
of course, death and its weariless prompter, time.
Even here sexual symbolism has an expressive role to
play. So far we have noted only the benign face of the
vital impulse as Horace perceived it. But what lyricist
has more to say than he on the banes of the unrestrained
will? In love, in politics, in music, incautious surrender to the impulses spells disaster. Hence, his
symbols, given the requirements of context, can turn
back upon themselves and bode not creative, but ruinous
élan.

Nonetheless, it is death itself, by its setting of
limits to each and every pullulation of the life force,
that determines the ultimate function of the symbolism
in the Odes. Through the symbolism, that is to say,
Horace sets life against death in his lyrics, the resources of creativity against the abyss. There can be
little doubt as to his immediate inspirator. Though
with profoundly different results, he duplicates the
method of Lucretius: Venus is antithesized once more

10

to the plague, love to death. But whereas Lucretius
looked philosophically to the life of the universe for
solution to the anguish of mortality, Horace, the incomplete Epicurean, could see only the abyss.[8] I do
not suggest that he surrendered abjectly to the terrors
of time. His music, he proudly affirmed, would live
on. But he knew nothing so well as the beauty of life
and the bleakness of extinction.

The uniqueness and power of the Odes lies in the
insoluble tension between these two perceptions, and it
is the work of the symbolism to articulate the tension.
In the process, nothing of the best that has been discovered in Horace is disturbed. Rather, among other
gains, his sensibility, beyond merely engaging, becomes
commanding, his devotion to his art grows more profound
and even his humor acquires fresh suppleness and depth.
But a deeper seriousness also sets in and, with death's
slow conquest over love, even an irremediable pathos.
The result, far from the platitudinous charm with which
he has been credited, is a personal lyric as fresh,
daring and immediate as any ever composed.

Since poetic analysis through sexual symbolism has
scant basis in classical studies, a further word on
rationale and method seems inevitable. If, as I intend
to show, there are figures, passages and even entire
lyrics that yield no real sense outside the symbolism,
we are obliged to conclude that Horace consciously
utilizes symbolic imagery in these particular places.
This being so, we may proceed on the hypothesis that
wherever he employs the same or like imagery, the use is
similarly conscious and, indeed, likewise aimed at illu-
minating meaning. The critic's task in offering a sym-

11

bolic reading thus consists in, first, seeking out the
operative pattern of symbolic images and, thereupon,
explicating the latent access of meaning.

Seeing that Freud has taught us how to proceed,
the first aspect of the task presents little difficulty.
It is at the same time well to keep in mind that, though
such a study as this would be unthinkable except for
Freud, it is not indebted to his authority. We have
seen that the language of sexual symbolism was familiar
to the poets from time immemorial. Moreover, if we
place the results of our brief search among Horace's
predecessors alongside Henderson's findings in Aristophanes, we discover that virtually all of our poets'
symbols derive from previous usage. Thus, if Freud
has opened a way to the ancient poets, it is a path
which they themselves first laid down.

As for the second part of the task, it is clear
that, at least on a poem-to-poem basis, a conscious symbolism allows us to aim at nothing less than intended
meaning. To some, as is well known, poetry scarcely admits of such a thing. My conviction is that this makes
better dogma than theory. I would also insist that no
approach to artistic creation is more sensible than to
impute the unmistakable to the author's intention.
Hence, where sexual symbolism is concerned, when a luna-
tic rides a hydrogen bomb to earth in Doctor Strangelove,
or when Charlotte Haze coos coaxingly to Humbert Humbert
(resolved to turn down her lodgings, but about to behold
Lolita for the first time), "Now let me show you the gar-
den," or, on another level, when some dismal genius of
Madison Avenue has us ponder whether a gentleman should
offer a lady a Tiparillo, the authors cannot but intend

their obvious implications. In Horace, the symbolic constructs are often similarly pellucid. But even where they are not (and sometimes they are but elements of a larger puzzle), we may assume on grounds already laid down that, being no less consciously composed, they are equally intentional. My method in deriving the intention will consist simply in a search for the ways in which the symbolic content of any given lyric enhances the poetic argument. The result, if the search prospers, will open onto the author's intention. I cannot promise such felicity throughout; but, even if it eludes me at every turn, the failure will not lie in the method.[9]

A further major consideration hangs on the claim for conscious intention. In the main, the ensuing study will not be at all psychoanalytical in approach. It is not that I have any severe quarrel with that method. On one occasion, in fact, I shall invoke it myself, and that precisely because no other approach is adequate to the difficulty at hand. But in all else, we shall content ourselves with the operations of an uncommon consciousness.

CHAPTER TWO
THE LOVE ODES

Horace was an orderly lyrist. Each of his first
nine odes is dressed in a distinct meter, the nine comprising all of the major verse forms to follow. Similarly, the nine furnish the essentials of the work's
sexual symbolism. As was Horace's evident plan, the
fifth and ninth odes would suffice for a preview of the
symbolism, but, in view of its superb corroborative
effect, I shall also include the eleventh in my own
introduction.

We start with the ode that is in every way the
cornerstone of the love lyrics (1:5):

> Quis multa gracilis te puer in rosa
> perfusus liquidis urget odoribus
>   grato, Pyrrha, sub antro?
>   Cui flavam religas comam,
>
> simplex munditiis? Heu quotiens fidem
> mutatosque deos flebit et aspera
>   nigris aequora ventis
>   emirabitur insolens,
>
> qui nunc te fruitur credulus aurea,
> qui semper vacuam, semper amabilem
>   sperat, nescius aurae
>   fallacis! Miseri, quibus

intemptata nites. Me tabula sacer
votiva paries indicat uvida
    suspendisse potenti
       vestimenta maris deo.

    What slender lad, steeped in liquid
perfumes, caresses you beneath the pleasant grotto, Pyrrha, amid an abundance
of roses? For whom do you bind back your
yellow hair, simple in your elegance? Ah,
how often shall he lament perfidy and the
altered gods and, all inexperienced, gape
at the seas made rough by black winds,
who now, credulous, enjoys you as a thing
of gold and, ignorant of the faithless
breeze, hopes you will be ever free, ever
amiable! Unhappy are those for whom you
glitter untried. As for myself, the temple wall shows by a votive tablet that I
have dedicated my dripping garments to
the puissant god of the sea.

I urge anyone interested in exploring the hundred nuan-
ces of art that make this ode the triumph that it is to
consult Ernest A. Fredricksmeyer's exemplary study.[1]
Here we are interested solely in the sexual images.
    One conclusion is certain. The identification of
Pyrrha with the sea is absolute. A second, in the
light of Fredricksmeyer's work, is irresistible. She
represents no particular individual--nor even, I would
add, a particular persona, like a Lydia, Lyce or Chloe--
but universal woman in her sexual nature. It follows,
then, that Horace uses the ode, among other purposes,
to establish the sea, or more generically, water as emblematic of woman in her sexuality. Although the identification of Pyrrha with the sea is properly metaphori-
cal, I shall make bold to use the term symbol. Bolder

still, I will maintain that the ultimate symbolic value
of the sea/water image--though it may not carry quite
to the level of sense in this ode--is of the vagina itself. There is no need to argue the point at this
juncture. Lyric after lyric, both within the erotic
odes and, even more signally, without, will bear out
the association abundantly.

More salient perhaps is the wind symbolism. The
callow gracilis puer, says Horace, will be stunned at
the seas made rough by black winds--at Pyrrha transformed from submissive mistress to raging fury. To be
sure, the image evokes a wider range of the vehement
emotions as well. The main point is that it suggests
passion. Now let us turn to aurae fallacis a bit further on. The youth, being ignorant of the faithless
breeze, trusts that Pyrrha will be always free and
amiable. Here the wind image designates sexual desire
pure and simple. Fully spelled out, the meaning is that,
like the sea, whose openness and amiability can instantly change in a shift of wind, so will Pyrrha's avail-
ability and receptiveness be altered by shifts of sexual
desire. At least provisionally, then, we may cite the
ode as furnishing archetypes of sexual images for the
Odes, the sea suggesting the female in her universal
sexual nature and wind implying passion in general and,
specifically, sexual passion.

But Horace did not intend the ode as a mere index
of sexual imagery. Rather, the poem attains a great
measure of its power and depth as a precise result of
such imagery. We have not yet taken note of the symbolism in the very first verses. The surface picture is
of a stripling lad wooing Pyrrha, surrounded by roses,

16

in a grotto. But also at the surface is the odd word
urget. It means "caresses", as I have rendered it for
convenience, only with a fair amount of charity. Fundamentally, the word signifies a physical, thrusting
motion. Meanwhile, of all possible vaginal symbols,
the cave or grotto is among the most certain. Hence,
the opening verses suggest, indeed nearly depict, sex
in the process of enactment. Now, to comprehend the
ode on any level requires the understanding that, at
the beginning, the smooth youth is much in command of
things. Several scholars have pointed out that even
the word order gracilis te puer is calculated to suggest
Pyrrha's captivity. The image of copulation offers nothing to disturb the impression. Indeed, there is something in the bald physicality of urget which implies
even a cool arrogance on the boy's part, which in turn
causes Pyrrha to appear the more thoroughly captive.

Then comes revolution. Urget becomes flebit as
the youth's casual mastery turns into panic. Figuratively, he drowns and passes utterly away beneath the
forces of female sexuality. The image, no less elemen-
tally powerful than the Charybdis figure in the Odyssey,
is possibly even more so in that, unlike Odysseus (and
Horace), the lad does not escape. Yet, till Fredricksmeyer, this was an ode which, as it were, literary history had entitled, "To a Flirt".

The eleventh ode of Book I Horace addresses to
Leuconoe ("Ingenuous"):

Tu ne quaesieris, scire nefas, quem mihi, quem tibi
finem di dederint, Leuconoe, nec Babylonios
temptaris numeros. Ut melius, quicquid erit, pati,

17

> seu plures hiemes, seu tribuit Iuppiter ultimam,
> quae nunc oppositis debilitat pumicibus mare
> Tyrrhenum: sapias, uina liques, et spatio brevi
> spem longam reseces. Dum loquimur, fugerit invida
> aetas: carpe diem, quam minimum credula postero.

> Stop asking, Leuconoe, how long your life or
> mine. And enough of horoscopes. Only the gods
> can know. Much better to take things as they come,
> whether Jupiter has many winters in store or none
> but this, which wears away the Tyrrhenian Sea
> against the facing cliffs. If you would be wise,
> strain your wines and tailor long hopes to the
> short run. Time flies as we talk. Seize the
> day. Tomorrow may never come.

The bold image of the sea being worn away--more literally, having its strength sapped--against the opposing
cliffs is comprehensible only on the symbolic level.
In keeping with the sea symbolism of the Pyrrha ode, it
means simply that time saps the female's sexual power.
It thus assumes a functional role in the poem's argument,
paving the way for the final summons to youth's pleasures. The following image, being more personal, is
even more sexual. Vina liques, advises Horace, "Strain
your wines". On first impression, this admonishes
Leuconoe to stick to the things she knows, like this
humble household chore, rather than posit grand meta-
physical questions. But the whole point of the poem
comes in the last line, carpe diem, and one does not
"seize the day" by keeping busy at kitchen tasks. One
exploits one's youth. One makes love.[2] Symbolically,
therefore, the liquid image in vina liques, following
as it does immediately upon the sexually suggestive
water imagery of line five, is wholly sexual. Horace's

adjuration to the girl is to perfect herself sexually, obviously by close devotion to the task of love.

In the entire four books there is no poem whose unity and meaning rests more squarely on sexual symbolism than the Soracte ode (1:9):

> Vides ut alta stet nive candidum
> Soracte, nec iam sustineant onus
> silvae laborantes, geluque
> flumina constiterint acuto.
>
> Dissolve frigus ligna super foco
> large reponens atque benignius
> deprome quadrimum Sabina,
> O Thaliarche, merum diota.
>
> Permitte divis cetera, qui simul
> stravere ventos aequore fervido
> deproeliantes, nec cupressi
> nec veteres agitantur orni.
>
> Quid sit futurum cras fuge quaerere et
> quem Fors dierum cumque dabit, lucro
> appone nec dulcis amores
> sperne puer neque tu choreas,
>
> donec virenti canities abest
> morosa. Nunc et campus et areae
> lenesque sub noctem susurri
> composita repetantur hora,
>
> nunc et latentis proditor intimo
> gratus puellae risus ab angulo
> pignusque dereptum lacertis
> aut digito male pertinaci.

You see how Soracte stands white in layered snow, how the laboring woods fail to sustain their burden and the rivers stand still in the bitter cold. Dissolve the cold, piling logs high upon the fire, O Thaliarchus,

> and draw out lavish draughts of vintage
> Sabine. Leave the rest to the gods, for,
> as soon as they have calmed the winds
> which battle on the fervid sea, neither
> cypress nor ancient ash are longer shaken.
> Do not ask what the morrow brings, but
> count as gain whatever sum of days fortune
> gives. Spurn not sweet love, my lad, nor
> the dance, so long as sullen old age keeps
> its distance. Now is the time to make for
> the campus, the squares, the soft whispers
> at nightfall, the trysting hour, and now
> the tell-tale, delighted laugh from a se-
> cret corner of a girl in hiding, the pledge
> plucked from the arm or the unresisting
> finger.

One of the most deadly obstructions to a grasp of the
ode's unity and sense has been the impression that its
setting abruptly changes. The season at the beginning
appears to be winter, at the close spring. The ode is
set not in the year's seasons, however, but in the seasons of life. Thus, if the opening scene is regarded
as symbolizing old age, the ode instantly begins to
assume form. Thaliarchus, the young addressee, is also
better regarded in the abstract, that is, as every young
man rather than any specific youth.[3] It follows that
our Youth is first warned of the inevitable fact of old
age and finally urged to make for the scenes of love
now, while he is young. No sentiment could be more
Horatian.

Meanwhile, the most expressive symbols remain unde-
tected. In the opening tableau we see woods laboring
under a weight of snow, together with frozen-over waters.
Waters we already know suggest the female genitalia,
while the trees intimate the phallus. The mountain
(following Horace's lead as surely as Freud's) is em-

20

blematic of either sex. And all are beset with burdens
symbolic of old age. The difference between the stanza
without and with awareness of the symbolism amounts, I
suggest, to the difference between vivid description in
verse and fully realized poetry.

Next, Thaliarchus is urged to pile his fire high
and let the wine flow generously. Again the liquid
(female) image and again (through the logs) the tree
image, this time combining to impart tacitly the same
message which Horace makes explicit in the final ten
verses: make love.

Of all segments of the poem perhaps the third
stanza is the most obscure. The seasonal difficulty
especially obtrudes. How can a winter sea be fervid?
Once more symbolism is the key. As soon as passion
ceases to rage over the ardent female, Horace is inti-
mating, the phallus ceases to be vexed. The stanza thus
corroborates the first, warning Thaliarchus anew that
sexual powers ebb to nothing with age.[4]

Symbolism even manages to enrich the beauty of the
close. Commenting on the intricate word-placement in
the last seven lines and particularly on the way in
which various interlacing groupings suggest brilliant
vignettes of their own, Gilbert Murray says, " . . . I
am not sure that there is not something in 'intimo
gratus'--'delightful in the deep'."[5] I am certain that
there is, especially seeing that intimo modifies the
symbolic angulo. Finally, rarely does Horace achieve
so fine a blend of delicacy and drama in his symbolic
effects as in the final two images. Symbolically, both
bracelet and ring are vaginal. By suggestion, then,
the young lady is weak to resist the surrender not

merely of pledges, but of love itself.

It is plain that these three lyrics, comprising as they do Horace's first offerings on the theme of love, combine to promise a sort of poetic disputation on the subject. Two stand together as carpe diem odes. More than that, it is obvious that Leuconoe is the abstract counterpart of the abstract Thaliarchus, the universal young woman, whom, like every youth, Horace urges to practice love with single-minded intent while time allows. Yet the Pyrrha ode, the work's first love lyric and all but its most powerful, serves warning of love's terrific perils, especially for the young. We shall find that the remaining erotic odes conspire in an absorbing expansion of this dialectic. We shall also find a resolution. But if the reader's leading interest is, like my own, Horace's poetic art, our chief discovery will be that the most consistent and meaningful vehicle of expression throughout it all is sexual symbolism.

One does not read far into Horace's love odes before he realizes that none of his Grecian inamorate ever lived, much less loved. Such undisguised artificiality, I suspect, is a main reason why we have not yet appreciated the depths to which these lyrics sound the erotic experience. True, there is not and cannot be in such verse the kind of intensity that burns in the poetry of Catullus. Nowhere in the Odes do we find the awesome devotion that Catullus conferred upon Lesbia or the pathos which is its result. Still, Horace does not lack passion. He creates a range of emotion, sometimes paralleling Catullus, from delicate tenderness to rage, from prayerful submission to extravagant masculine pride.

Like Catullus too, he is as acquainted with the coarse
as with the sublime. And, concerning the sublime, when
things are going right in the mirrored world of Horace's
amours, there is a taste of love's joys as exquisite as
anything anywhere in the pages of his gifted predecessor.

Meanwhile, compensating for any lack of "real" experience in Horace is an intrinsic strength which
Catullus' poetry by its very nature must lack. This is
poetic detachment. It is owing to this quality that
Horace's love lyrics realize a unique expressiveness,
and clearly, the detachment originates in nothing other
than the insubstantiality of his inamorate. He thus
freed himself to become a persona among personae in a
many-sided representation of the love encounter which
might explore the erotic experience itself and particularly its various stresses. What we find in Horace,
then, is a calculated study of love, detached and objective. Not the least benefit of such disengagement is
that it permits the full participation of his fine sense
of the absurd, so that the lover might emerge as Horace
essentially saw him: victim of a madness vital to his
sanity. In short, Horace's perspective on love is objective, rational and, by and large, amused. It is
everything that Catullus' is not.

Thus, if his love lyrics have less than wholly to
do with real bodies in the living night, it is by design. It is notable that, where they dealt with the
erotic, Lucretius and Vergil worked by the same design,
that is, by objective scrutiny of love's variegated
powers. But neither, in my judgment, explored the love
experience so deeply or delicately as Horace. I would
even suggest that, among the Romans, all that was not

23

said by Catullus on the subject of love is available in Horace. It is no small thing.

One final comparison to Catullus is particularly appropriate to this study. In the Lesbia cycle sexual symbolism is fairly hard to come by. It simply found scant place in poetry of such direct personal passion. But in a poetry committed from the start to the indirect and the universal, symbolism, the device of the indirect and the universal, is, besides congenial, almost an inevitable medium of expression. But again, artifice and, not the least, the artifice of symbolism need not entail any loss of power. The Pyrrha ode is powerful. Would it be quite so were the sea not Pyrrha's symbol? Or, for that matter, would it be more so had the lady actually lived?

We will resume on the note with which we first started (and whither we shall return), a Horatian farewell to love (3:26):

> Vixi puellis nuper idoneus
> et militavi non sine gloria;
>   nunc arma defunctumque bello
>   barbiton hic paries habebit,
>
> laevum marinae qui Veneris latus
> custodit. Hic, hic ponite lucida
>   funalia et vectes et arcus
>   oppositis foribus minaces.
>
> O quae beatam diva tenes Cyprum et
> Memphin carentem Sithonia nive,
>   regina, sublimi flagello
>   tange Chloen semel arrogantem.

>   Till now, I have been a vital match
> for girls, and I have campaigned not with-

out glory. Now this wall which keeps the
left side of seaborn Venus shall have my
arms and my lyre that is finished with
war. Here, here place the shining torches and the crowbars and the bows that
were a menace to bolted doors. O you who
possess blessed Cyprus and Memphis, free
of Sithonian snow, queen, just once flick
the haughty Chloe with your high-raised
whip.

Horace is as fond of playing little tricks upon himself
as upon his reader. One of his favorite devices, as
here, is to undermine a solemnly made resolution at the
first right opportunity. Plainly, he is bidding farewell
to love only because of his poor success with Chloe.

Though this piece never acquires anything like the
tensions of the Pyrrha ode, Horace evidently meant the
two to be considered together. As Wili noted,[6] this
lyric stands fifth from the end of Book III, just as
the Pyrrha ode stands fifth in Book I, and if critics
have established anything beyond question in Horatian
art, it is that arrangement is crucial. Perhaps the
major advantage of comparing the two is the discovery
that the later poem disowns the seemingly deep resolution of the Pyrrha ode as fully and insouciantly as, in
its own course, it undermines its own. It is Horace's
final way (for he had intended Book III to be the last
of the _Odes_) of telling what the intervening lyrics
have confirmed over and over again, that the lessons of
love cannot be learned, but only repeated.

The imagery is rather different from anything we
have seen so far. For Freud the symbolism of the house
was vaginal. So is it for Horace, not only in the
paraklausithra, but otherwise. Again proof is best

25

left to the poetry itself. Here the torches, crowbars
and bows, all means of forcing entry through barred
doors (themselves obviously symbolic) are unmistakably
phallic. Chloe alone (so the ode would suggest) withstood the onslaught. And so for Chloe there remains a
lash of the--phallic--whip. But, again, though Horace
may reserve the final thrust for himself, it is love
that claims the last word.

An even more elegant admission of failure at love's
game and an imagistically more germane reprise of the
Pyrrha ode comes at the close of <u>Albi</u> <u>ne</u> <u>doleas</u> (1:33,
13ff.). Horace advises the poet Tibullus not to grieve
too much over unrequited love, since love knows no
reason. He offers several cases in point, concluding
with his own recent dilemma:

> Ipsum me melior cum peteret Venus,
> grata detinuit compede Myrtale
> libertina, fretis acrior Hadriae
>   curvantis Calabros sinus.

> Take myself; when a more honorable
> love was yearning for me, who held me
> fast in chains of love but slave-born
> Myrtale, wilder than the Adriatic where
> it shapes Calabria's rounded bays.

<u>Curvantis</u> <u>Calabros</u> <u>sinus</u> is a lyrical triumph. The
literal import itself consists of a handsome piece of
imagery. Yet there subsists a second imagery, founded
in familiar dictionary meanings, which, once noted, puts
the primary out of mind: the ripeness of breasts, belly,
thighs.[7] And that is scarcely all. Once feel the sen-
suousness of melody and meter--above all, the long,

voluptuous lingering on curvantis--and the apprehension
of female sensuality becomes entire. At the same time,
the last six words, particularly when related to the
Pyrrha ode, gives acute new insight into the power of
beauty to seduce. Like Pyrrha, Myrtale possesses all
of the wild might of the sea to corrode and destroy.
As with Pyrrha, therefore, this should constitute ample
grounds for rejection. But such a response would require rationality, and the ode is a testimonial to precisely the opposite force in human nature. Seeing that
the last is virtually made flesh by the undulations of
curvantis Calabros sinus, we can scarcely mistake what
it is precisely for which Horace's rational powers of
resistance are no match.

Such tensions between the negative and positive in
love, between the irrational and the rational and, on
the highest level, between the destructive and creative,
lie at the core of Horace's love lyrics. We will also
find, just once, a resolution of all tensions, together
with a statement of love's positive force that is at
once modest and wonderfully exalting. There also awaits
to be reconciled to the whole a melancholy expression
of love's final futility. But little of it, including
the terms of the tensions themselves, comes clearly
into focus without a careful reading of the images.

Working together with the tensions just noted
there is one further consideration, the consciousness
of mortality, ever critical to Horace's perspective on
love. In particular, the pervasive theme of love's
seasonability is rooted in the lessons of mortality.
We now turn to a cycle of odes centering on that theme,
starting with an address to one of love's uninitiates

(1:23). The symbolic values will be mostly familiar:

> Vitas inuleo me similis, Chloe,
> quaerenti pavidam montibus aviis
>   matrem non sine vano
>   aurarum et silvae metu.
>
> Nam seu mobilibus veris inhorruit
> adventus foliis seu virides rubum
>   dimovere lacertae,
>   et corde et genibus tremit.
>
> Atqui non ego te tigris ut aspera
> Gaetulusve leo frangere persequor:
>   tandem desine matrem
>   tempestiva sequi viro.

> You avoid me, Chloe, like a doe
> searching for her timid mother in the
> trackless mountains, not without empty
> dread of the breezes and the forest.
> For she trembles in heart and limb,
> whether the arrival of spring has rus-
> tled in the quivering leaves or green
> lizards have parted the brambles. And
> yet I do not pursue you to shatter you,
> like a vicious tiger or a Gaetulian
> lion. Quit your mother once and for
> all being ripe to follow a man.

The ode is an elegant reductio ad absurdum. On the
literal level it argues that, like the doe, Chloe fool-
ishly exaggerates the perils that surround her. For the
doe that milieu is denoted by aurarum et silvae. How do
these apply to Chloe? By established symbolic values
they easily translate themselves into her sexual fears.
The reductio operates here as well: like the doe's,
these fears are also groundless. The second stanza is
a beautiful expatiation on the sexual suggestion of

aurarum et silvae. Not only does the detail of the
rustling foliage reinstate breeze and tree (desire
and the phallus) with exquisitely heightened effect,
but the detail of lizards parting the brambles in-
escapably intimates sexual intercourse. There is nothing to dread in any of this, the poet assures the
girl; it is but the intention of nature and time.
Even without the symbolism, admittedly, the ode is a
gem, but a gem half lit.

When Horace turns a second time to the subject
of the virgin young (2:5), the symbols work just as
cannily to evoke the adolescent female mind. After
admonishing himself that Lalage (who is metaphori-
cally a heifer) is still too young for sex, he continues (5ff.):

> Circa virentis est animus tuae
> campos iuvencae, nunc fluviis gravem
> solantis aestum, nunc in udo
> ludere cum vitulis salicto
>
> Praegestientis. Tolle cupidinem . . .

> Your heifer's mind is on the
> pastures; now she finds relief in the
> streams from the heavy heat, now she
> yearns terribly to romp with the
> calves in the wet thickets. Check
> your desire . . .

Praegestio is an extremely strong expression of desire.
Added to the fact that gestio unaided denotes powerful
yearning, the prefix prae- is intensive. The prefix
also carries the temporal suggestion of being before-

29

hand. Meanwhile, it is clear, wet thickets symbolize
at once female and male sexuality. Lalage's potent
but precocious desire to romp there with the young
males--can poetry be more delicately expressive of
inchoate sexual desire? Iam te sequetur, Horace continues (1. 13), "soon she will follow you". The pre-
diction is far more compelling coming out of the symbolic, rather than the simply literal meaning of
verses 5-9.

Once more (3:12) Horace tries his hand at the same
sort of thing, with results that remarkably anticipate
Freudian insight. Complaining that girls are permitted
no release for their erotic yearnings, Neobule day-
dreams of her yet-unloved beloved, dwelling on his
physical (athletic, hunting) accomplishments. Her
thought closes thus (10ff.):

> . . . catus idem per apertum fugientis agitato
> grege cervos iaculari et celer arto latitantem
>   fruticeto excipere aprum.

> . . . [he is] skilled to spear stags
> fleeing across open ground in a startled
> herd and quick to take the boar lurking in
> the dense thicket.

Literally, her beloved is sure of his prey whether in
open or overgrown terrain. There is a certain sexual
implication even on this level. But the ode fails to
take us very deeply into Neobule's yearnings until we
note the covert sexuality of these closing images:
spearing, the heavy thicket, the lurking boar, the taking (literally excipere means "to take to oneself",
while the boar is a very archetype of male sexuality).

30

Some of the symbolic values are obviously transferred,
and Neobule is the last to recognize whereof she thinks.
But it is precisely that innocence which compels her
deepest longings to surface in disguise.

Though, on the whole, Horace is gentle and solici-
tous toward the very young, we misread the poetry if we
fail to note one further trait of the imagery. In all
three odes response to emerging sexuality is couched in
suggestions of animality. With Neobule and Lalage especially, but even with Chloe, considering her suggested
fear of voracious beasts, scant doubt is left that Horace intends to make a definite and even approving tie
between sexuality and the animal nature. For the animal
within to waken is natural and inevitable, and, as he so
gently admonishes Chloe, it must be accommodated. So
too must the beast without--the rushing bull (1:3) of
the Lalage ode, Neobule's boar and even, duly modulated,
Chloe's "tiger" and "Gaetulian lion". But Horace ap-
proves, as we shall see, essentially for the reason that
time is on the side of the young. Moreover, he makes
one further stipulation before extending his full blessing. Chloe is _tempestiva sequi viro_, and, as for Lalage,
Iam te sequetur. The woman must subordinate herself to
the man.

That this is no light matter with the poet is
proved in one of his most famous odes. _O fons Bandusia_
(3:13) closes with this symbolic statement:

> Fies nobilium tu quoque fontium,
> me dicente cavis impositam ilicem
> saxis, unde loquaces
>   lymphae desiliunt tuae.

> You too will become one of the
> famous founts through my celebrating
> the oak imposed upon the sloping stones
> whence leap your babbling waters.

Though this poem and, indeed, this stanza carries more
than a sexual import, sexuality is fundamental to everything. The importance of the stanza is apparent in that
it constitutes nothing less than a characterization of
the Odes' essential poetry. Its full meaning must await
a fuller context. But our acquaintance with the symbolism already enables us to say that Horace identifies
himself as, prominently, a love poet and, more than that,
a love where the male dominates.

 With Lalage and Chloe, as we have seen, he insinu-
ates a propriety in female subordination from earliest
times. The other side of the coin is male domination
asserted early. This he tends to stress by spelling out
the consequences where the young man fails to impose
himself decisively. Pyrrha's young lover is a cardinal
case in point; and it is doubtless a measure of Horace's
convictions on this matter that he revisits the theme
only three odes further on (1:8). Lydia, he charges, is
destroying Sybaris by loving him. The youth no longer
joins his companions in athletics or military exercises,
but, like the transvestite Achilles before the conflict
at Troy, hangs back beneath a woman's gloating affections. The two pieces combine to issue a grave warning
early in the Odes. However arch the tone of the Lydia
ode, there subsists a firm implication of personal ruin,
specifically of emasculation. Pyrrha's lover, meanwhile, is headed toward a similar end, but through an experience of more violent emotions. The combined message

is clear: whether by soft means or hard, the young
lover will come to harm under the domination of a stronger will.

What of eros and the aged? Age forbids love, says
the bard--for women. At least, he never brings himself
to apply the argument, which must surely apply to both
sexes if to either, unreservedly to the male.[8] Where he
pleads advanced age to protest his own disinterest in
love (4:1), for instance, he merely ends by confessing
desire for a boy. The unrequiting lad is then (4:10)
plaintively lectured on the tolls which time exacts--
tolls which the ardent poet has already long paid--but
only the aged woman is asked, and not kindly, to renounce
Venus. If ever there was a proposition that cried out
for the peculiar dialectical subtleties of an Horatian
ode for its justification, it is this; but such an ode,
alas, there is none.

Horace announces his view, all fire and fury, in
his most savage lyric (1:25), just two entries after his
most tender:

> Parcius iunctas quatiunt fenestras
> iactibus crebris iuvenes protervi,
> nec tibi somnos adimunt, amatque
>   ianua limen,
>
> quae prius multum facilis movebat
> cardines. Audis minus et minus iam:
> 'Me tuo longas pereunte noctes,
>   Lydia, dormis?'
>
> Invicem moechos anus arrogantis
> flebis in solo levis angiportu,
> Thracio bacchante magis sub inter-
>   lunia vento.

33

cum tibi flagrans amor et libido,
quae solet matres furiare equorum,
saeviet circa iecur ulcerosum,
    non sine questu

laeta quod pubes hedera virenti
gaudeat pulla magis atque myrto,
aridas frondes hiemis sodali
    dedicet Hebro.

    Brazen youths less often now rattle
your closed shutters with raps and blows
and rob you of no sleep, and the doors
which once swung often on easy hinges hug
the threshold. Now less and less you
hear, 'Do you sleep, Lydia, while I, your
own, die for you whole nights through?'
Instead, a degenerate hag, you will weep
at the arrogance of womanizers in your
deserted alley, while the Thracian wind
runs mad on moonless nights, when your
searing desire and lust, like that of
mares in heat, will rage around your corrupted heart, and you will complain that
merry youth rejoices too much in green ivy
and fresh myrtle and consigns dry leafage
to the Hebrus, the mate of winter.

First, reverting to the primary stuff of this study, let
us look at the sexual images and their effects. The
closed shutters, the once-much-frequented doorway and
the deserted alley are all by intimation vaginal, and
each tells a differently shaded but simple tale. Also
the forbidding water imagery at the close is feminine
and sexual in implication. Through the epithet "mate of
winter" (mate of old age, mate of death), the gelid river
suggests in a collective way the aged, sexually defunct
female. Here is the withered Lydia discarded, sapless
leafage into a deadened stream--both images thus ex-

pressing a nullity of vital waters.

More crucial is the wind imagery. Wind, as we have seen, can suggest sexual desire in any context. Here the wind raging like a maenad (<u>bacchante</u>, <u>1</u>.11) in the abandoned alley--itself the starkest vaginal symbol of all--<u>becomes</u> Lydia's sexual desire. Maddened, huge desire indeed, and (<u>magis</u>) it grows steadily larger. Moreover, according to ancient popular belief, it was the wind that impregnated mares. We are thus led by free, yet remorselessly linked association to the climactic image of the mare in heat.[9] At first it strikes us as the crowning indignity as well, and, doubtless, Horace would not have minded our questioning not only his taste, but even his humanity. Revulsion is what he wants. Only, he would have argued, the inhumanity is expressly Lydia's, not his own.

For, animal desire, as he has made plain, is not improper to those in their prime. It is even somehow rational, since it comes forth naturally in the scheme of things and, to take the argument to its inevitable conclusion, also has its natural function. Animal passions nursed into old age, however, are monstrous, especially where, as Horace foresees in Lydia's case, they dominate over every other faculty and impulse. In other words, Lydia has long past foresworn all hope of rational control in her life, hence of all distinctive humanity, by abandoning herself to the animalistic urge. This Horace finds execrable and thus his ferocious scorn.

There is also enormous effect in the positioning of the poem, just two entries after the Chloe ode. That dealt with the season of initiation into love, this with the time for renunciation. But it is the pathetic dirge

of Quintilius that falls between which most unifies the
ensemble.[10] Quintilius is dead, Horace mourns, and not
even Vergil's piety and gift of music can bring him
back again. What is lost to time, then, is lost forever.
As it is precisely the claims of time that Lydia resists,
we can perceive the cause of Horace's scorn even more
clearly. If Vergil, a paragon of civilized virtue, must
bear time's imperatives, who is Lydia to refuse? A
little reflection shows that such rebellion bulks even
larger than any positive attachment to animal lust in
explaining her debasement. Her essential corruption is
that she cannot accept the human condition, and this in
turn entails an ultimate void of rationality and of
humanity.

Nothing would be more absurd than to separate what
is gained from the positioning of an ode from its proper
effect. The whole impress, then, is of a dread of decline urging the mind to monstrous irrationalities.
Psychologically and philosophically Horace never runs
deeper. On both counts his debt to Lucretius is plain.
More closely to home, meanwhile, let us not lose sight
of the large expressive role played by the symbolism.

Lyce too as superannuated crone is subjected to
Horace's contempt, but with her the tone is lighter,
more mocking than splenetic. The ode, in fact, does not
attain its proper significance except in relation to an
earlier, highly sophisticated address to the same lady
(3:10), where Horace, playing the shut-out lover, im-
plores her affections. The context there returns us to
grounds familiar from the Pyrrha ode: Horace at once
testifying to the mindless power of love and seeking to
establish a measure of independence from it. Symboli-

cally, the poem is a festival:

> Extremem Tanain si biberes, Lyce,
> saevo nupta viro, me tamen asperas
> porrectum ante fores obicere incolis
>   plorares Aquilonibus.
>
> Audis, quo strepitu ianua, quo nemus
> inter pulchra satum tecta remugiat
> ventis, et positas ut glaciet nives
>   puro numine Iuppiter?
>
> Ingratam Veneri pone superbiam
> ne currente retro funis eat rota;
> non te Penelopen difficilem procis
>   Tyrrhenus genuit parens.
>
> O quamvis neque te munera nec preces
> nec tinctus viola pallor amantium
> nec vir Pieria paelice saucius
>   curvat, supplicibus tuis
>
> parcas, nec rigida mollior aesculo
> nec Mauris animum mitior anguibus.
> Non hoc semper erit liminis aut aquae
>   caelestis patiens latus.

> Even if you drank from the remote
> Tanais, Lyce, and were wife to a savage,
> you would be sorry to expose me, stretched
> full-length as I am before your cruel
> doors, to the north winds that haunt this
> place. Do you hear with what groanings
> your gate and the grove planted within
> these lovely precincts re-echo to the
> winds, and how Jupiter glazes the fallen
> snow beneath the open sky? Put aside this
> arrogance so repugnant to Venus, lest the
> rope run backward on the turning wheel.
> Your Tuscan father did not beget you to be
> as inaccessible to your lovers as Penelope.
> O, though neither gifts nor pleas nor the
> violet-tinted pallor of lovers nor the fact

>   that your husband is smitten with a
>   Thessalian harlot bends you, be kind
>   to your suppliants, you who are no
>   softer than a rigid oak nor gentler
>   of mind than an African serpent. These
>   ribs will not endure your threshold and
>   the waters of heaven forever.

If the symbolism of the adamantly closed doors is routine, me . . . porrectum ante fores obicere . . .
Aquilonibus introduces a startling new proposition:
Horace has cast himself as nothing other than the rejec-
ted penis erectus. The suggestion is too graphic to be
mistaken or avoided. Cruel doors shut him out porrectum
(the word is more a graffito than a description) to
suffer the north winds, i.e., his ungratified desires.
Next arrives a more routine set of intimations. While
on the surface complaining merely that it is terribly
cold outside, the second stanza offers on the symbolic
level an object warning from nature that female and male
alike are subject to the tortures of sexual privation:
gate and grove moan in the wind. Meanwhile, the frigidity mixed with the loveliness (pulchra tecta) of the
locale holds a mirror to Lyce herself. It is of course
the frigidity which prevails--amidst further shocks of
symbolism. Neque . . . te curvat, Horace complains:
nothing bends Lyce; she is as hard as the stiff oak, as
cruel as the serpent. Unmistakably, she has now herself
become tantamount to the penis erectus. Whatever one
thinks of such imagery, its suggestion that Lyce in her
adamant determination to resist is fully a match for
Horace's rigid insistence, is wonderfully functional.
Nothing could better express the impasse of wills
(Horace's plea for kindness is obviously forlorn) and,

therefore, the futility of further remonstrations. Horace's final, sensible admonition thus develops smoothly from all that precedes.

There remains only the question of symbolic balance. If Horace plays the part of the phallus at the beginning only to defer to Lyce, does he reclaim that role at the close? I think he does. The closing admonition, after all, amounts to non hic semper porrectus manebo. It is quite an ode.

If he has not already, the poet gets the last word with Lyce the next time around (4:13). On first impression, it may seem that we are dealing with a different lady, so greatly has she changed. But Horace could scarcely have intended us to understand by his triumphant opening, "The gods, Lyce, have heard my prayers; yes, they have heard, Lyce," any other than his tormenter of the past.

Though grown old, she still wants to appear beautiful and exults in wine, men and song. But Cupid shuns her, Horace mocks symbolically, no differently than he does old men (9f.): transvolat aridas/quercus et refugit te; "he flies over dried-out oaks and shrinks from you." We note, thus, another parallel between Lyce and the phallus. Far from stubbornly resisting love, however, she is now all eagerness but is, like any defunct love-member, scorned by the god of love. In this massive peripateia, of course, lies the ironic resolution of her former will to resist. Still, Horace does not let matters rest there. In the closing lines we get a last, pathetic look at the phallic Lyce. The fates, says Horace, have preserved her (once nec rigida mollior aesculo):

> . . . possent ut iuvenes visere fervidi
> multo non sine risu
> dilapsam in cineres facem.

> . . . that ardent youths, full of laugh-
> ter, might look upon the torch crumbled
> into ashes.

Nor does even that close the matter. Once again a detail of organization compels special notice. This stands last of the love lyrics in the last book. Important as that position is, we must take care not to overrate it. Books I-III comprise the essential structural unit of the _Odes_. Intriguing nonetheless is the question why Horace chose this particular piece to round out the love lyrics in the expanded edition. Technically, the explanation is clear enough. Seeing that the poem is symbiotic with the first Lyce ode, it reaches back, so to speak, into the earlier group to pull the fourth book into closer physical union with it. By virtue of the same symbiosis the ode also manages to evoke the whole span of Horace's erotic career, which is right for a terminal poem. But why this terminal tone? Here, I think, we must look to mood rather than art for an explanation.

The Horace of the final book is skeptical of love. Of Phyllis, his "last love" (4:11) he asks only song to dispel dark cares, this after the poem's beginning, with its wine, garlands and festivity--not to mention the fine erotic suggestiveness of lines 15f.--give promise of Venus in the old manner.[11] His major ardency would seem to be homosexual (4:1; 4:11), but even this lacks conviction. Above all, these odes are troubled with

consciousness of advancing age. Hence, whether consciously or not, the closing image of the Lyce ode may
reflect, besides all we have seen, regret for his own
faded potency as well.

In any case, the objective and detached study of
love that the erotic odes of Books I-III keep rigorously
intact takes a subjective and none too happy turn in
Book IV. Nor is this trivial. I will not suggest that
the poet's evident melancholy here ever came to dominate
the spirit of the whole, but, as we shall see, it will
grow even more prominent before it settles into
perspective.

Still a third time Horace attacks an aged devotee
of sex (3:15). Everything that is important is comprised in the following (8ff.):

> . . . filia rectius
> expugnat iuvenum domos,
>   pulso Thyias uti concita tympano.
> Illam cogit amor Nothi
>   lascivae similem ludere capreae . . .

> . . . it is more proper for your daughter
> to assault the homes of youths like a
> maenad thrilling to the beaten drum. Love
> of Nothus forces her to frisk about like a
> sportive she-goat.

First and last, we must appreciate the superlative boldness of this pair. Soul of corruption that she was,
even Lydia had the decency to await attention within her
own walls. But not even this comparison quite captures
Chloris' (the mother's) brazenness. Horace's subtle
statement of the case features the daughter. Like a

maenad Pholoe storms the homes of young men--not Nothus'
home exclusively, we note, though her whole justification
is that she does love Nothus. As for Chloris, we must
infer that, even without that justification (without
amor!), she engages in the same extraordinary enterprise.
This is ineffable prurience. For its part, the imagery
intimates nothing less. The storming of homes in the
service of love is the proper work of men. So much for
the ladies' aggressiveness. Symbolically, besides, it
is the work of the phallus. So much, Horace implies,
for the ladies.

It is evident that even in his amatory prescriptions
for young and old love's irrational power lies at the
center of Horace's thought. Four additional odes will
further reveal his dedication to that theme. Though we
will indeed see more of love's capacity to insinuate and
destroy, the poet dwells for the most part on its seductive powers short of catastrophe.

First an ode which, I feel, has been radically
misunderstood, though not primarily through any insensi-
tivity to the sort of symbolism we have been following
(1:19):

Mater saeva Cupidinum
        Thebanaeque iubet me Semelae puer
et lasciva Licentia
        finitis animum reddere amoribus。

Urit me Glycerae nitor
        splendentis Pario marmore purius;
urit grata protervitas
        et vultus nimium lubricus aspici.

In me tota ruens Venus
        Cyprum deseruit, nec patitur Scythas

42

　　　et versis animosum equis
　　　　　Parthum dicere nec quae nihil attinent.

　　　Hic vivum mihi caespitem, hic
　　　　　verbenas, pueri, ponite turaque
　　　bimi cum patera meri:
　　　　　mactata veniet lenior hostia.

　　　　　The cruel mother of the Cupids and
　　　the son of Theban Semele and wanton License
　　　command me to turn my mind again to loves
　　　that are ended. The radiance of Glycera,
　　　who glows purer than resplendent Parian
　　　marble, burns me; her charming forwardness
　　　burns me and her face too smooth to hold
　　　the gaze. Venus deserts Cyprus to rush
　　　upon me with all her might, nor does she
　　　permit me to speak of the Scythians or
　　　the Parthian, brave when his horse is
　　　turned in rout, nor of anything that is
　　　not to the point. Place live turf here,
　　　lads, here place boughs and a flagon of
　　　two-year-old wine. The victim slain, she
　　　will come more gently.

Bennett's comment on mactata hostia is, "Since no victim
has been mentioned, and since only bloodless sacrifices
were made to Venus, the phrase is probably equivalent to
sacro peracto, unless the poet is playfully alluding to
himself." Horace is surely alluding to himself. He
will be the "victim", and he will be "slain"--by wine.
And, save for one detail, that is all. I suggest that
Venus' might is more keenly captured by in me tota ruens
than first meets the eye. The verb ruo, which almost always denotes a massive force in motion, occurs memorably
in connection with love on another occasion. The unripe
Lalage is not yet ready to bear the weight of the bull
ruentis in venerem (2:5, 3f). Venus' singleminded

assault here is best understood in similar terms. Figuratively, that is, Horace is being subjected to sexual
assault by the goddess of love. There is nothing he can
do or say, especially nothing he can say about retreat
(10ff.), to avert it. Hence, he submits, with only wine
to soften the blow.

'Thus understood, the ode is not only Horace's
drollest testament to the irrational might of love, but
perhaps his most powerful. And it is important to see
that such force is required to give full effect to the
ode's opening proposition. If reason is anywhere tan-
gent to the erotic experience, it must be where the love
affair is broken off. This happens, we would say, for
a reason. For some reason. Where exhausted desires
rekindle themselves, then, irrationality has either
carried all in its path--it is not for nothing that
Dionysus is explicitly present (l. 2)--or else the desires have not been exhausted. Either way, mindlessness
conquers completely, and it is precisely this utter
puissance of the irrational that the ode must capture
if it is to fulfill its promise. Hence the imagery's
daring and strength is nothing too much.

Passions' renewal also provides the subject of
Donec gratus eram tibi (3:9); an ode sharply different
from Mater saeva Cupidinum in texture and tone, but in
substance nearly identical:[12]

> 'Donec gratus eram tibi
> nec quisquam potior bracchia candidae
> cervici iuvenis dabat
> Persarum vigui rege beatior'.

> 'Donec non alia magis
> arsisti neque erat Lydia post Chloen,

multi Lydia nominis
    Romana vigui clarior Ilia'.

'Me nunc Thressa Chloe regit,
    dulcis docta modos et citharae sciens,
pro qua non metuam mori,
    si parcent animae fata superstiti'.

'Me torret face mutua
    Thurini Calais filius Ornyti,
pro quo bis patiar mori,
    si parcent puero fata superstiti'.

'Quid si prisca redit Venus
    diductosque iugo cogit aeneo,
si flava excutitur Chloe
    reiectaeque patet ianua Lydiae?'

'Quamquam sidere pulchrior
    ille est, tu levior cortice et improbo
iracundior Hadria,
    tecum vivere amem, tecum obeam libens'.

    'As long as I was pleasing to you and
no youth was more welcome to enfold your
snowy neck in his arms, I lived more blest
than the king of Persia'.
    'As long as you burned no hotter for
any other and Lydia was not second to
Chloe, I, Lydia, flourished vast in re-
nown, more noble than Roman Ilia'.
    'Now Thracian Chloe rules me, versed
in sweet measures and skilled with the
lyre, for whom I would not fear to die,
if only the fates spare her soul and allow
her to live'.
    'Calais the son of Thurian Ornytus
now burns me with torch communal, for
whom I would twice endure to die, if only
the fates spare the boy and allow him to
live'.
    'What if our old love returns and
forces us, now parted, beneath the brazen

45

yoke, if golden-haired Chloe is thrust
out and the door is opened again to
spurned Lydia'?
  'Though he is lovelier than a star
and you lighter than cork and more tem-
pestuous than the wanton Adriatic, with
you would I love to live, with you glad-
ly die'.

We may start with a question which, to my knowledge, has
never been posed before. Why in the midst of an elegant
contest of wits does the youth (Horace?) abruptly offer
a renewal of love? While we are at it we may also wonder at the dazzling incoherence within which he couches
his offer. In lines 16f. we are led to believe that
love is a force imposed utterly from without; in the next
breath it becomes entirely a matter of choice. Formally,
we must remember, the situation calls for suave verbal
thrust and parry. Has the lover at this point, excited
and perplexed, forfeited victory for sake of the prize?
If so, what is it about Lydia that he cannot resist?
And what does Chloe lack?

    With Glycera it was beauty and a "charming forward-
ness" that captivated Horace. The case is scarcely different here. Candidae cervici conveys Lydia's beauty,
while, as we shall see, a grata protervitas is her most
winsome gift. First, however, let us note a quality
which Lydia seems conspicuously to lack. Chloe is
dulcis docta modos et citharae sciens. Now, a young man
who sees the ideal human state in an exotic blessedness
(1. 4) must find intense appeal in such aesthetic accomplishments. Chloe, we might even hazard, is his ideal
match. Why, then, does he promptly and so unceremoni-
ously offer to be rid of her? Perhaps we have already

asked enough questions to agree at least that jealousy,
the ode's surface emotion, is an inadequate answer.

Let us look deeper into Horace's characterization
of this pretty pair. The most striking aspect of the
imagery is that twice, in the door image of 19f. and
the water imagery of the final stanza, the young man is
symbolically·associated with the feminine. Nowhere in
the Odes, in fact, is the prototypal Pyrrha more distinctly recalled than in improbo iracundior Hadria.
Such symbolism comes as no great surprise, since the
most striking thing about the youth himself is his com-
plex emotional dependence (donec gratus eram tibi; me
nunc Thressa Chloe regit), which by conventional standards conveys effeminacy. His inclination to aesthetic
delicacy likewise carries a conventional feminine tonal-
ity. Conversely, Lydia possesses the more masculine
sensibility. She feels the more immediate urge of the
flesh, and certainly she better understands its potency.
She it is who introduces and then, countering his submissive me . . . Chloe regit with the wonderfully phallic
and egalitarian me torret face mutua, triumphantly enlarg
es upon the suggestion of sexual fire, which is to say,
the realities of sexual desire. This constitutes her
protervitas. And, obviously, it is grata, seductive.
Chloe is forgotten, reason abandoned. What has transpired is simply that her sensuality has brought home to
the youth all that she had been to him in the past and
all that, despite Chloe's superior refinement, he must
have again. It is rather typical Horace. Not only are
there similarities to the Glycera ode, but we have seen
seduction from a melior Venus before (1:33). The great
thing about this ode is that the seduction, or better,

the transfusion of fire, is enacted before our very
eyes.

Perhaps only Horace would have thought of expressing love's power to sap the mind of reason by means of
an ode which itself slips steadily into unreason as it
unfolds. It is impossible to sound more soberly sententious than do the first two verses of Integer uitae
(1:22):

> Integer vitae scelerisque purus
> non eget Mauris iaculis neque arcu . . .

> The man of pure and perfect virtue
> needs no Moorish javelin or bow . . .

or more blissfully enchanted than in the last two:

> . . . dulce ridentem Lalagen amabo,
> dulce loquentem.

> . . . I will love my sweetly laughing,
> sweetly speaking Lalage.

Nor is there a trace of logical development between the
two points to help bridge over the discordancy. The
man of moral purity, Horace begins, needs no weapons
wherever he goes. By way of proof he reports that a
stupendous wolf fled him in the Sabine wood while, un-
armed and carefree, he wandered singing of Lalage.
Logically, it was his moral integrity that saved him.
We might therefore expect a claim that his goodness will
continue to guard him wherever he goes. Even the assertion that his music will do so would make tolerable

sense. Instead (17ff.):

> Pone me pigris ubi nulla campis
> arbor aestiva recreatur aura,
> quod latus mundi nebulae malusque
>   Iuppiter urget;
>
> pone sub curru nimium propinqui
> solis in terra domibus negata:
> dulce ridentem Lalagen amabo,
>   dulce loquentem.

>   Place me in lifeless plains where
> no tree is reborn in the summery breeze,
> in that quarter of the world which
> clouds and a malevolent sky oppress:
> place me beneath the too closely veering
> chariot of the sun in a land denied habi-
> tations: I will love my sweetly laughing,
> sweetly speaking Lalage.

I will not suggest that this diaphanous nonsense is to
be dismissed in favor of a deeper stratum of meaning.
Rather, the collapse of logic is deliberate and functional. What logic, after all, is there in rapture, and what
can the ode mean to express if not the spell of enchantment in which Lalage has Horace bound?

    There subsists a figurative reading nonetheless
which both discloses a thread of unity in the ode and
aptly enlarges upon its intrinsic nonsense. We shall
take the latter effect first. Horace will persist in
loving Lalage not merely in regions where there is no
love, but, through the symbolism of tree and home, no
sexual parts wherewith to love. This crowns the integ-
ral nonsense, of course, but at the same time it ex-
presses nothing if not chastity, which provides a needed

link to the high moralism of the opening verses. It also links on to the symbolism there, which likewise intimates asexuality. Weapons, we have noted in _Vixi puellis_, carry definite phallic implications. Here, then, the virtuous man who needs no javelin or arrow wherever he goes translates symbolically into the chaste man who needs not the phallus. Beginning and end thus come together. The wolf episode also conforms easily to the theme of chastity. We shall find in _Velox amoenum_, 1:17, (where, incidentally, Horace also claims a tutelary force in his virtue and where the theme of chastity too is prominent) that the wolf almost certainly stands for brute sexuality. The whole paradigm thus squares nicely with the rest in expressing an invincible integrity in Horace's sexual virtue. This is the more impressive in that he undergoes his trial in the (symbolic) forest while Lalage (_1_.10) was very much in his thoughts.

Does the poem finally argue, therefore, that chastity keeps a man safe from harm--if only the harm that derives from sexual temptation? Not quite, for Horace's chastity, even as it figures in this poem, is thoroughly in doubt. In lingering lovingly on Lalage's speech and laughter and especially in pronouncing each separately _dulce_, the closing verses betray that her appeal is emphatically to the senses after all. Also, the vow _amabo_, despite its context, cannot but connote desire. All of this cuts deeply into the posture of chastity, leaving the Horace we have come to know from, among other sources, the other Lalage ode. How then to explain the poem? It is a transport, a piece of love-struck logic that propounds at its heart a sexual interest so prepossessing as to put sexual interest to rout. The manifest rational void is the whole point.

In each of the last three lyrics, as in the Myrtale ode, Horace (if the young lover of 3:9 is indeed Horace) succumbs almost without struggle to love's seductions. What, then, of his earlier admonitions, unvoiced yet palpable, to temper love with caution? His further admonition, obviously, is that this is not always possible. What is to insure the lover against misery in these instances? The Odes contain no answer, unless, for his own part, it is Horace's claim to be a ward of Faunus (1:17, 1ff.; 2:17, 29f.). The reader, presumably, may be another.

It may seem that Horace, even for Horace, is playing too freely here with his own ground rules. Yet with these odes he merely confesses that love is by its nature a seduction and that, short of excluding it altogether, reason cannot keep its risks entirely at bay. Neither does a proclivity to seduction wholly cut off reason, however.

For sheer seductive force Barine (2:8) has no peer in the Odes. Yet, for good reason, Horace is mortally cautious. Barine is a near doublet of Pyrrha. Each is gifted in perfidy, and both devastate those innocent enough to succumb to their perilous beauty. Innocence is the operative term. Corresponding to the naive puer of the Pyrrha ode are the iuvenci (1. 21) and mariti novi (1. 24) who are Barine's especial victims. Hence it is Horace's experience--a compound of his knowledge of the femme fatale and self-knowledge--which saves him from harm. Nonetheless, the Odes remain anything but a manual of survival in the game of love. For if it is experience that saves, what is it that saves the uninitiated from experience?

Barine's ode is somewhat deceptive. It would appear to center on her irremediable corruption, but the more fundamental subject proves to be love's own indifference to morality. Hence, not only the beloved's but the lover's moral integrity invites close attention. It is on these grounds that the poem strikes out in a new direction from the Pyrrha ode. Pyrrha's young lover, we gather, is unlikely to survive her treachery. But Barine's lovers cannot have enough of it. Though a notorious liar, she need but mint a fresh vow to "shine forth more beautifully" (5f.). Worse, it profits her to swear falsely on her mother's ashes, the stars, the heavens entire and the gods themselves (9ff.). Yet it is plain that the blame is not Barine's alone. Her lovers too have lost their scruples. How else might her transparent lies profit her? Horace adds (16ff.):

> Adde quod pubes tibi crescit omnis,
> servitus crescit nova, nec priores
> impiae tectum dominae relinquunt,
>   saepe minati.

> Add that the whole of youth grows
> for you, a new band of slaves grows for
> you, nor do the former ones, for all
> their threats, quit the house of their
> wicked mistress.

The notice that the youths are no better than Barine at keeping their vows is further evidence of shared corruption. Notable too is a fine ironic correspondence between this (second from last) and the second stanza: just as Barine's beauty grows amidst fresh vows, so

does her helpless horde of lovers burgeon amidst broken
ones. Finally, there is a subtle, but inevitable and
utterly germane hint of phallic excitation in the repeated crescit. It is, after all, the state of abject
sexual desire upon which the poem turns. It is this
which gives Barine her powers over men and robs them of
their moral self-mastery. Hence, if the whole of youth
"grows" in response to her overpowering beauty, the
verb cannot fail to verify its connotation without fail-
ing the poetry.

The same and more is expressed in the ode's imagistic centerpiece. After exclaiming that Barine profits
by unspeakably perjured oaths, Horace laments (13ff.):

> Ridet hoc, inquam, Venus ipsa, rident
> simplices Nymphae ferus et Cupido,
> semper ardentis acuens sagittas
>   cote cruenta.

> I swear, Venus herself smiles at
> this, the simple Nymphs smile and Cupid,
> ever honing his glowing arrows on the
> bloody stone.

There is a remarkably controlled and meaningful narrow-
ing of focus within this stanza. Till we reach ferus
Cupido it rests on the blithe amorality of the divinities of love. Though the god shares in the gaiety, his
amusement dissolves almost instantly into a mien of
fierce concentration. Straightaway, his point of focus
becomes ours, the arrows, or rather, for us it becomes
the arrows' puissance. As surely as the bloodied stone
reflects their past conquests, their glowing heads tes-
tify to new ones to come. If there is a phallic symbol

anywhere in Horace, it is these mindlessly ardent and
rapacious, all-triumphant arrows. It is to them, obviously, that we must look for love's moral pertinency.
But how ironic a symbol it is even beyond that! For
their victims in the ode are surely not the all-triumphant Barine, but her lovers, and, conversely, their
powers--ultimately, the whole of phallic appetency--are
no one's possession but her own. This is to say a bit
more than that Barine's powers depend on erect masculine desire. They are that desire, which is why her
lovers, who are in their entirety nothing more than
that desire, are the sheer nothings (iuvenci) that the
ode describes. We have spoken of love's emasculatory
threat before, but nowhere is it made so vividly real,
especially in its moral application, as here.

Thus far we have gathered that love, while a natural and irresistible force, bids fair to make a fool of
the lover if it does not ruin him entirely. But, set
against Horace's judgment on love in the Odes at large,
this becomes an inadmissibly dark state of affairs.
There is scant notice of love's dangers, for instance,
in the carpe diem odes. Hence, unless Horace is to risk
serious self-contradiction, he must somewhere indicate
a way beyond love's perils. He makes three such suggestions, one cynical, one sublime and one his intended
last word on love. We shall take them in that order.

Cum tu Lydia Telephi (1:13) continues to baffle
scholars. For its major portion it parodies romanticism,
only to break, for all appearances, into a romantic
pledge of perpetual devotion at its close. Compounding
this evident problem of unity is the fact that Horace is
not given to romantic devotion, least of all with the

concupiscent Lydia. Finally, the task of analysis is
also somewhat complicated by a heavy influence of literary models.

　　The first part of the ode must be understood against
the background of Sappho's famous phainetai moi kēnos
and Catullus' imitation (Cat. 51). Horace starts with
the complaint that Lydia's incessant praise of Telephus
affects his liver, causing it to "burn and swell with
choking bile," causing him also to blanch and to weep
secretly, betraying his inward agony. These figures at
once recall the poems of Sappho and Catullus and strike
up a parody of their tremulous romantic sentiment.
There the rival is seen as one made divine by the privi-
lege of the beloved's presence, while the lover sits by
in helpless rapture. Here the lover is sketched as an
insensate boor (9ff.) who nearly mutilates Lydia with
his lovemaking, while, for all practical purposes, the
pathetic transport of Sappho and Catullus is reduced to
the image of hepatic tumescence. Through parody, in
short, the sublime is made vulgar, spirit becomes flesh.
Certainly, there is nothing here inconsistent with Horace's relationship to Lydia in general, nor is the intimation that love is, by nature, a sensual thing untypi-
cal of Horace. Then (13ff.):

　　　　Non, si me satis audias,
　　　　　　speres perpetuum dulcia barbare
　　　　laedentem oscula quae Venus
　　　　　　quinta parte sui nectaris imbuit.

　　　　Felices ter et amplius
　　　　　　quos irrupta tenet copula nec malis
　　　　divulsus querimoniis
　　　　　　suprema citius soluet amor die.

> If you will listen to my advice, do
> not hope that he will remain constant who
> savagely wounds those sweet kisses which
> Venus has imbued with the quintessence of
> her nectar. Thrice happy and more are
> those whom an unbroken connection holds
> together and whom love, never sundered
> by vicious quarrels, does not release
> till the last day.

The _irrupta copula_ which Horace offers is indisputably
a perpetual bond of love. But what is this _copula_
amoris if the suggestion of romantic devotion seems out
of place? Must it not be perpetual copulation? Immediately the surface tone of exaltation withers into a
cynicism that is all the more devastating for being so
prettily masked. The point at hand is that the cynicism
chimes well with the ironic tones of the first three
stanzas, and so makes a unity of the ode. As for Lydia,
there is cause for hostility from Horace's side. What
response, in fact, is more to be expected from a Horace
to a soul of carnality like Lydia who presumes to mock
him with praise of a brutish rival?[13] Catullus, we will
recall, showed an equal arrogance toward Ipsithilla
(Cat. 32) with no apparent provocation. Indeed, that
poem may have served as another of Horace's models, for
the differences between _novem continuas fututiones_ (Cat.
32, 8) and _irrupta copula_ as we construe it are merely
those that inspired imitation would create.

In any case, we have not yet penetrated to the
ode's full cynicism. The imagery suggests that even the
jealous rage of the first stanza--_fervens difficili bile_
tumet iecur--is feigned and, like _irrupta copula_, also
masks a state of sexual lust. We have already seen (in

a Lydia ode) that the liver is the seat of lust, a lust
indeed that "rages" (1:25, 13ff.):

> . . . cum tibi flagrans amor et libido
> quae solet matres furiare equorum
> saeviet circa iecur ulcerosum . . .

Here, meanwhile, _fervens_ and _tumet_ have a phallic to-
nality practically identical to that of _ardentes_ and
crescit in the Barine ode; and _difficili bile_ also
easily accommodates itself to a phallic interpretation.
Putting this preliminary hint of sexual arousal together
with that of perpetual coitus at the close, we may conclude that the poem is a secret derision of Lydia from
first to last (the mockery again responding to her
mockery of Horace), with Horace's single commitment
throughout being a naked prurience. The ode thus lights
one evident way beyond love's perils. Offer and solicit
nothing but the flesh.

Horace's one pervasively elevated tribute to love
is the idyllic ode to Tyndaris (1:17). As usual, there
is more to the poetry than lies on the surface, where
Horace tenders an affection almost "Platonic". Still,
nothing in the ode saves the emotions, for all their
dignity, from hollowness. What we are given is merest
reverie in the classical mode. But the performance is
matchless.

Horace extends to Tyndaris the blessings of peace
and the muse, with peace expressed as both immunity from
violence and the active serenity that derives from divine benevolence. "The gods protect me," he sings (13f.)
"to the gods my goodness and my muse are dear." Does he

harbor sexual designs? Suggestively, yes, but only amid suggestions to the contrary.

Horace blends the worlds of beast and man into an Arcadian unity. Faunus preserves his she-goats from the fiery heat and rainy winds (2ff.), while they wander through the groves safe from lizard and wolf. From the images of heat, wind, grove and lizard, we gather that their safety extends to sexual immunity from their "rank mates" (l. 17) as well. As for Tyndaris (17ff.):

> Hic in reducta valle Caniculae
> vitabis aestus . . .
> > nec metues protervum
>
> suspecta Cyrum, ne male dispari
> incontinentis iniciat manus . . .

> > Here in this hidden vale you will
> avoid the heat of the dog-star . . .
> nor will you fear lest the violent Cyrus,
> distrusting you, malignly lay heavy hands
> on one so poorly matched to him . . .

Like the flocks, she too will be preserved from both the literal heat of the day and the figurative heat of passion; and Cyrus evidently stands to her as does the wolf to the she-goats in the earlier lines. Even the landscape is gathered into the ambience of continence, for if in reducta valle suggests anything in regard to sex, it is chastity.

Still, Tyndaris will sing of love, of "Penelope and radiant Circe striving for the same lover" (19f.). It will not harm to note in passing the never-varying centrality of the male. More to the present point, a

positive representation of erotic desire has now clearly surfaced. Just before these lines, meanwhile, in the
poem's central stanza, the same suggestion comes through
at once more directly and more subtly:

> Hic tibi copia
> manabit ad plenum benigno
> ruris honorum opulenta cornu.

> Here the opulent abundance of the
> honors of the countryside will flow
> plenteously for you from the kindly
> horn.

We ought first appreciate the artistry of the "word picture": Horace beautifully encloses his description of
the opulent cornucopia with its component words, copia
and cornu. The symbolism is equally graceful. Being
both horn and hollow, the cornucopia as a sexual symbol
embraces both sexes.[14] This evocation of oneness exquisitely suits the exalted spirit of the ode. Seeing
that the horn is meant for Tyndaris, however, the phallic implication inevitably comes to dominate, simultaneously heightened and softened by the suggestions, respectively, of inexhaustibility and kindliness (benigno,
l. 15). At last, then, a tangible evidence of an erotic
intention, but all in good time and all gently.

As a way past the horrors of love, the ode clearly
counsels civilized retreat. But all is not well.
Granted, those two features that entail rational pri-
macy--the abhorrence of violence and the cultivation of
the muse--must be felt central to Horace's concept of
positive love. We may even say that the ode does not
violate that concept on the basis of anything that it

contains. It is what is absent that rings false, and
what is absent, of course, is time. In Horace, the
authentic Horace, the only possible disengagement from
time is death. The ode must therefore finally be
accounted a dreamful flight from the poet's own convictions.

Horace's most complete statement on love, fittingly
one of the carpe diem pieces, is the little ode to Lyde
(3:28):

> Festo quid potius die
>   Neptuni faciam? Prome reconditum,
> Lyde, strenua Caecubum
>   munitaeque adhibe vim sapientiae.
>
> Inclinare meridiem
>   sentis ac, veluti stet volucris dies,
> parcis deripere horreo
>   cessantem Bibuli consulis amphoram.
>
> Nos cantabimus invicem
>   Neptunum et viridis Nereidum comas;
> tu curva recines lyra
>   Latonam et celeris spicula Cynthiae;
>
> summo carmine, quae Cnidon
>   fulgentisque tenet Cycladas et Paphum
> iunctis visit oloribus
>   dicetur; merita Nox quoque nenia.

> What better can I do on the festival
> of Neptune? Bring vigorously forth, Lyde,
> the stored Caecuban, and mount an assault
> on wisdom's stronghold. You see that the
> noon declines, and yet, as if the swift
> day stood still, you hesitate to hurry
> forth from the storehouse the cask linger-
> ing since the year Bibulus was consul. We
> will sing in turn, I of Neptune and the

60

> green-haired Nereids; you shall chant
> on your curved lyre Latona and the
> arrows of swift Cynthia; in our final
> song she who with yoked swans visits
> Cnidos and the gleaming Cyclades and
> Paphos shall be celebrated; night too
> has its fitting song.

Till Pöschl, this had remained among the least noted of
the love odes.[15] Yet, its mere position and dramatic
occasion suffice to prove that, for Horace, it is a
crowning work. Not only does it stand as the last love
poem in the original edition of three books, but the
festival of Neptune which it celebrates links it directly to Pyrrha and the first love ode. Great issues are
entailed. Most important, Horace's ironic prayer there
to potenti maris deo for salvation from love is now
countered, indeed superseded, by a positive turning to
love in the god's name. Nothing here contradicts his
tendency to wariness in matters of the heart. Pyrrha
and the perils of love which, as elemental woman, she is
made to represent, remain what they were. Horace's parting assurance, nonetheless, is that love--specifically,
love informed by the mind's highest faculties--can be a
wondrous force for the good.

Symbolic effect is nowhere more fertile. We have
already seen that the choice of setting is not haphazard.
This feast day, moreover, far more than a simple anni-
versary of the ancient sea god, is seen through the symbolism it symbiotically shares with the Pyrrha ode to
celebrate female sexuality. Even as a unit of time it
is affected by the symbolism. Given especially the
stress laid on its swift, relentless passage, the day
comes to represent the female's--here, Lyde's--sexual

life-span. And the day is on the wane. Closely linked
with this, the choice vintage which Lyde is ordered to
bring forth represents her sexual favors. _Pace_ Commager,
wine in the _Odes_ most often intimates love and, most
directly, the female's love. Set, as the ode firmly
sets them, in the context of time, the symbolic projec-
tions thus combine to create an intensely new (yet
familiar) situation: Lyde's favors are long-kept and
exquisite; yet, though her sexual life-span steadily
narrows, she hoards them still; the time to spend them
is now.

Neither does Horace's imperious tone throughout
these verses signify nothing. He clearly wants his
Lyde subservient. The symbolism throws his will to dominate into the sharpest relief possible. Lyde must not
merely suppress every inclination to intellectualism,
but this _together_ _with_ producing her sexuality. In sum,
Horace demands an emotional partner, not, an intellec-
tual companion, but, manifestly, a partner whose emotions, as a very condition of the relationship, he can
manage. Intellectualism aside, Lyde is everything that
Pyrrha is not. We must conclude that, to Horace, such
are the least conditions upon which love can prosper.

From a modern point of view, it is true, he so far
manages to display little more than masculine arrogance.
And I shall be the first to concede that, as I understand the term, Horace was an extraordinary male chauvi-
nist. But, in fairness, that "little more" must be
appreciated, which, again, only requires an appreciation
of the Pyrrha debacle.[16]

In the balance of the ode sexual differentiation
exists only to be blended into one. The day, we have

noted, presses toward night, urging love. Yet, for all
of time's pressure, the lovers have time. Before love--
and before death--comes song, which, for its part, enacts the ancient human dialectic: Horace will sing of
the sea deities (again his sexual interest is symbolically emphasized), Lyde will respond in tones of chastity, but the last song will be Venus'. Astonishingly
deep poetic currents pervade the seeming simplicity.
We must take the last verse to mean that song of Venus
is suitable to night as being the time of love, all of
which nicely caps the dialectic of masculine overture-
feminine resistence-erotic consummation that has just
transpired in the singing. But, as the conclusion of
the "day" that inexorably wanes, night must intimate
death as well. Besides, though _nenia_ often signifies
merely "song", its primary meaning is "dirge". And,
finally, it is clear that death and dirge are as fitting
and inevitable a conclusion to the first half of the
poem as are love and nocturne to the second. Far from
a hopeless contradiction, however, the verse contains
a perfectly controlled ambivalence, which declares,
roughly stated, that the fitting music for night,
whether construed as the hour of love or the state of
death, is a song of love.

This is a note wholly new in Horace. For the first
time he displays a brave--we may even say romantic--
defiance of death. But by laws that inhere only in
poetry, the line's verbal sense is not yet its final
meaning. Owing to its occurrence after the caesura,
the phrase _Nox quoque nenia_ comprises a lyrical unit of
its own. So isolated and so final in the poem--and
conditioned by the mournful effect of _summo carmine_

enclosing the entire stanza together with <u>nenia</u>--its
heavy burden of death and lamentation is too powerful
emotionally not to make the final impression in the senses.[17] I would argue, however, that, final though it
is, this poetic triumph of death does not nullify Horace's show of courage, but simply transcends it with
the weight of reality that the ode is from the outset
courageous enough to recognize.

In any case, the true bravery lies elsewhere--in
the central portrait of two lovers who, though harried
to love by time, yet have the humanity to proceed at the
pace of a civilized inner tempo. More than bravery, we
find here an authentic and final triumph, if not over
time, then over the urgencies of instinct and passion
which time can make desperate. The presence of music is
of the essence. Horace's <u>magnum</u> <u>opus</u>, the fourth "Roman"
ode, makes a definitive bond between reason and the
muse.[18] But even without that majestic authority the
<u>Odes</u> impart in numerous ways that music is the mind's
highest form of expression. Here sex and death, the two
most powerful forces in nature, must wait for music, a
music which, by modulating desire, makes not just a harmony of mind and flesh, but a harmony which affirms
life's dignity.

The ode has more than answered one of our main
questions. The way past the perils of love consists in
a relationship wherein the threat of emotional ruin at
the hands of woman is well contained and, on a loftier
level, a relationship that is informed by the highest
human faculties. As elsewhere, Horace stops well short
of the heart's devotion. Love remains a simple natural
impulse. But, this once, he does not fall short of
genuine exaltation.

CHAPTER THREE
THE CARPE DIEM ODES

Just as no series of lyrics within the Odes sets
the principles of love and death more squarely in opposition than the carpe diem pieces, so no lyrical argument would seem more stable than that implicit in the
very title of the type: death demands that we love
while we may. Yet, Horace manages to baffle our expectations on both formal and substantive grounds. First,
as often as not, the entire protreptic to love is entrusted to symbolic expression. More important, with
the advent of the fourth book, the protreptic grows so
faint as to lose virtually all meaning. Eventually, we
shall find that Book IV presents us with a different
Horace in every major regard, but nothing marks the
change more decisively than this retreat from an enthusiasm that all but bears his name.

Though, as we shall presently see, the protreptic
begins to falter even within the primary edition, the
poet's commitment to it there remains nonetheless fundamental. It is well to recall that we have already sur-
veyed three sturdy specimens of the type in the
Thaliarchus, Leuconoe and Lyde odes. We resume with one
that would perhaps rate as the most robust of all were
it not for a weakness mistakenly perceived in the middle

65

THE GOLDEN PLECTRUM

stanza.[1]

     Solvitur acris hiems (1:4) opens with an announce-
ment of Spring, the season for sailing (l. 2), the season for plowing (l. 4). The promise of sexuality thus
placed emblematically in evidence is soon augmented by
a more conventional symbolization (5ff.):

> Iam Cytherea choros ducit Venus imminente luna,
>   iunctaeque Nymphis Gratiae decentes
> alterno terram quatiunt pede . . .

>   Now Cytherean Venus leads the dance be-
> neath the looming moon and, joined with the
> Nymphs, the lovely Graces trip the earth with
> rhythmic step . . .

Thus we arrive at the problematical centerpiece (9ff.):

> Nunc decet aut viridi nitidum caput impedire myrto
>   aut flore terrae quem ferunt solutae;
> nunc et in umbrosis Fauno decet immolare lucis,
>   seu poscat agna sive malit haedo.

>   Now it is fitting to bind glistening brows
> with fresh myrtle or any flower that the thawed
> earth breeds; now too it is fitting to make
> sacrifice to Faunus in shadowed groves, whether
> it is a ewe lamb or a kid that he demands.

Given the prelude, we naturally expect an erotic urgency
to attach to the repeated nunc--indeed, even to the repeated decet, since it subtly echoes the description of
the Graces (decentes) a moment before. Yet, Horace
seems to urge nothing more than a relaxed rural celebration, and, meanwhile, he presents a puzzle. Faunus'

66

festival occurs in February. Why honor him now?

For an explicit answer, the poet treats us to a
fresh surprise (13f.):

> Pallida mors aequo pulsat pede pauperum tabernas
>   regumque turris.

> Pale death beats with impartial foot at
> the huts of the poor and the palaces of the
> rich.

Every reader of Horace has understood how harshly this
imagery spoils, and is meant to spoil, the dance of the
love goddesses in the second stanza. The upshot, clearly, is that death urges us to love while we may, which
argument Horace now brings to bear on his addressee
(13ff.): life's brevity, O fortunate Sestius, forbids
us to entertain long hopes. Soon (Iam, l. 16) the
fabled Shades will claim you, and the barren house of
Pluto. The Iam tacitly seals the argument for erotic
urgency. Corresponding precisely to the Iam of line 5,
where Venus leads the dance, it signifies once and for
all that the dance is not forever, that love's season
is brief.

The ode then closes its circle with an overt resolution of the love motif (17ff.):

> . . . quo simul mearis
>   nec regna vini sortiere talis,
> nec tenerum Lycidan mirabere, quo calet iuventus
>   nunc omnes et mox virgines tepebunt.

> . . . and once you go there, you will win
> no lordship of the wine by the dice's cast,

> nor will you gaze marveling at youth-
> ful Lycidas, for whom all the boys now
> glow and the girls will soon grow warm.

We must not slight the effect of the nunc at the head
of the final line. Stressed by position, it concentrates notice on the love-object at this particular instant of his (and his lover's) life. And those lives,
we have been amply informed, are brief.

Now let us return to the central stanza and its
repeated nunc. Inarguably, evocations of erotic urgency by the same and similar words elsewhere make it all
the more imperative that these convey a like meaning.
Indeed, given the ode's precise concentric structure,
we should expect a powerful climactic progression converging from either side upon the middle: now, Sestius,
is the time for love; now death demands that you lay
claim to Lycidas; now is the time to garland the brow
and make sacrifice to Faunus. It requires symbolic
reading of the middle stanza to implement such a move-
ment. The symbolism of flowers and groves makes for an
evident start, but, unquestionably, the central meaning
must lie in the imagery of immolation. Nor, once we
realize that it is symbolic, is the meaning arduous.
Faunus (the Greek Pan) is the great phallic god of the
wild. Sestius may fittingly honor him with either a
ewe lamb or a kid; but, if the ceremony is figurative,
so too the victims. Figuratively, therefore, Sestius
may offer either a boy or a girl. And the "sacrifice"
will be Lycidas.

Immolation in a dark wood is an indisputably stark
metaphor for sexual initiation. Just how much ruthless-

ness is Horace recommending in the name of sexual gratification? No more, in truth, than allows the worshipper
to see beyond the pathos of any sacrifice. Lycidas'
victimization, that is to say, is requisite. Sestius,
his lover, must be resolved, must seize and pierce him
without further luxury of admiration if the sacred and
all too fleeting urgencies of desire are to be acquit-
ted. Such is homage to Faunus. And--decet.

In the brief, uncelebrated Aeli vetusto (3:17),
Horace burlesques Lamia's aristocratic pretensions by
tracing his ancestry to Lamus, a supremely barbarous
king of pre-Homeric times. The ode then concludes
(9ff.):

> . . . cras foliis nemus
> multis et alga litus inutili
>   demissa tempestas ab Euro
>   sternet, aquae nisi fallit augur
>
> annosa cornix. Dum potes, aridum
> compone lignum: cras Genium mero
>   curabis et porco bimestri
>   cum famulis operum solutis.

>   Tomorrow a storm let loose by the
> East wind will strew the forest with many
> a leaf and the shore with useless seaweed,
> if the aged raven, foreteller of rain, is
> not mistaken. Gather in dry firewood
> while you can: tomorrow, together with
> your household slaves freed from toil,
> you will minister to your Genius with
> wine and a two-month-old pig.

The last words cut a clever antithesis with the opening:
feast humbly with your slaves rather than upon your

69

aristocratic laurels. Meanwhile the injunction
Genium . . . _curabis_ produces the _carpe diem_ argument:
tend to your mortal self,[2] not your ancestry, to your
dwindling future, not your past.

And that is all, if we accept Horace's weather
divination at face value. But, obviously it takes the
antiquarian pieties of a Lamia to credit a crow's
meteorological competence. Nonetheless, a storm is on
its way. What sort of storm? The figurative storm,
surely, of old age. What is more, it will ravage
forest and sea--familiar symbols of sexuality. Gather
in wood for the morrow, the poet warns, and let the
wine flow. Symbolically, we are back in the Thaliarchus ode, save that the implicit erotic advice is addressed to an ostensibly older party.

In _Aequam memento_ (2:3), Horace weaves a fuller
argument on the _carpe diem_ theme. Never be prepos-
sessed by the circumstances of the moment, he warns
Dellius; for, even if they were to endure through life,
death's certainty (_moriture_, _l_. 4) renders them vapid.
An assurance, meanwhile, that such conditions likely
will change lurks in the opening advice to keep one's
poise both in prosperous and difficult times. Horace
thus works into the argument personal vulnerability to
fortune as well as to death. Death's inevitability,
however, is the leading thought, which, if it is a bit
understated in the opening verses, comes irresistibly
through at the close (21ff.):

> Divesne prisco natus ab Inacho
> nil interest an pauper et infima
>   de gente sub divo moreris,
>   victima nil miserantis Orchi.

Omnes eodem cogimur, omnium
versatur urna serius ocius
      sors exitura et nos in aeternum
        exsilium impositura cumbae.

It makes no difference whether you
linger beneath the sky a rich man sprung
from ancient Inachus or poor and of the
lowliest folk; you are a victim of piti-
less Orcus. We are all compelled to the
same destiny; the lot of each is shaken
in the urn, bound soon or late to issue
forth and place us on the bark headed
for eternal exile.

In short, the whole range of circumstances that might
predicate life--and we must remember that they are constantly shifting--pale before the one governing circumstance, death.

The state of mind which Horace recommends for
entertaining all of this is summed up by the opening
epithet, aequam (1. 1)--"balanced," "composed." Suggestions of reasonableness and good cheer also breathe
through the Latin. The behavior which he recommends
forms the substance of the middle three stanzas. For
our purposes, the first is the most striking (9ff.):

Quo pinus ingens albaque populus
umbram hospitalem consociare amant
      ramis? Quid obliquo laborat
        lympha fugax trepidare rivo?

Why do the huge pine and the white
poplar love to weave a welcoming shade
with limbs entwined? Why does the
fleeting water toil vivaciously along
its slanting course?

71

The questions are rhetorical. These beauties are here
to be enjoyed; hence, enjoy. But the questions are
fully fathomed only through the symbolism, which, if
evident enough, is not uncomplicated. Trees and waters
combine to present their usual erotic implication. At
the same time, one cannot fail to recognize a suggestion of the love embrace in the figure of the great
pine enmeshed with the delicate poplar.[3] But is this
the embrace of man and woman or of man and boy? Either
construction is admissible, surely, and therefore both
simultaneously.

Remarkably, the same set of images which fashions
such a tactful ambiguity nearly bowls us over with the
Priapean candor of <u>pinus</u> <u>ingens</u>. The audacity of the
pun is to be explained neither as mere caprice nor as
an exclamation of the passage's latent sexual meaning.[4]
Rather, its vaunting evocation of robust masculine
vigor, sounding an exceptional note in an argument that
turns on the feeble limits of human nature, represents
the poem's major affirmation of the life principle over
and against the stress of mortality.[5]

By the third stanza of this central triad, however,
the argument has backed down from such heights of
bravura (17ff.):

> Cedes coemptis saltibus et domo
> villaque flavus quam Tiberis lavit;
> cedes . . .

> You will withdraw from your
> boughten glades, from your mansion
> and your villa which the tawny Tiber
> bathes; yea, you will withdraw . . .

72

Glade, mansion and villa being all suggestively female, the symbolism of withdrawal speaks for itself. Still, all the more reason for Dellius to seize the day.

The differences between this and the Hirpinus ode (2:11) only tend to indicate their similarities. Dellius is absorbed in the present for reasons of his personal well being; Hirpinus, whose interests are communal, keeps a vigilant eye on the future; but time, reasons Horace, renders all such predilections and concerns equally inane. Subtly, as in the Dellius ode, fortune again enters as a complicating factor, for if chance can annul the present, how much more potent is it to unravel plans laid far into the future (1ff., 11f.)? Therefore, Horace advises, enjoy the passing hour.

Inquire no more into the plans of Spaniard and Scythian, Hirpinus, nor worry about life, since it demands but little (1-5). Youth flees, and beauty fades on the faces alike of flower and moon (5-12). Why weary your mind with counsels that are beyond its reach? Instead, let us recline beneath this tall plane or this pine and, perfumed and garlanded, let Bacchus dispel mordant cares (14-18).

But, as the imagery already suggests, Horace's interests range beyond mere wine-bibbing (18ff.):

> Quis puer ocius
> restinquet ardentis Falerni
>   pocula praetereunte lympha?
>
> Quis devium scortum eliciet domo
> Lyden? Eburna dic age cum lyra
>   maturet in comptum Lacoenae
>   more comas religata nodum.

73

> Which lad will quickly douse the
> cups of burning Falernum in the passing
> stream? Which will lure the shy wench,
> Lyde, from the house? Come, tell her to
> hasten with her ivory lyre, after bind-
> ing her hair in a tidy knot in the manner
> of the Spartan women.

The closing suggestion that Lyde is wanted strictly to
provide music, is, of course, merely the ruse to lure
her forth. Sex (certified by the epithet scortum) is
Horace's true purpose, just as it is sex which accounts
for his sudden show of haste. The symbolism makes for
the same conclusion. If we understand the "burning"
Falernum to signify sexual passion, then the poet's two
questions (18-22) coalesce and, in one fine stroke, the
symbolic waters (lympha, l. 20) becomes Lyde, as large
as life.

The major Lyde ode (3:28) aside, just two carpe
diem pieces remain in the primary edition. As it
happens, they mark the extremes of Horace's response
to the stress of mortality. In Tyrrhena regum progenies
(3:29), as we shall presently see, he blithely ignores
it. But in the Postumus ode (2:14), he leaves room for
little else:

> Eheu fugaces, Postume, Postume,
> labuntur anni nec pietas moram
>   rugis et instanti senectae
>   adferet indomitaeque morti:
>
> non si trecenis quotquot eunt dies,
> amice, places illacrimabilem
>   Plutona tauris, qui ter amplum
>   Geryonen Tityonque tristi

compescit unda, scilicet omnibus,
quicumque terrae munere vescimur,
    enaviganda, sive reges
        sive inopes erimus coloni.

Frustra cruento Marte carebimus
fractisque rauci fluctibus Hadriae,
    frustra per autumnos nocentem
        corporibus metuemus Austrum:

visendus ater flumine languido
Cocytus errans et Danai genus
    infame damnatusque longi
        Sisyphus Aeolides laboris:

linquenda tellus et domus et placens
uxor, neque harum quas colis arborum
    te praeter invisas cupressos
        ulla brevem dominum sequetur:

absumet heres Caecuba dignior
servata centum clavibus et mero
    tinget pavimentum superbo,
        pontificum potiore cenis.

    Alas, Postumus, Postumus, the fleet-
ing years glide by, nor will piety retard
wrinkling or pressing old age or indomitable death, not even if you seek, my
friend, with three hundred bulls each
passing day to appease tearless Pluto,
who shuts thrice-ample Geryon and Tityos
within that gloomy stream, which all who
feed on earth's gifts must surely sail,
whether we shall be kings or resourceless
farmers. In vain will we shun bloody
Mars and the rugged waves of the hoarse
Adriatic, in vain through the autumn will
we guard against the south wind so bane-
ful to our bodies: we must see the dark
Cocytus with its sluggish flow and Danaus'
infamous offspring and Sisyphus doomed to
long labors: you must leave your land,

75

> your home and pleasing wife, nor will
> any of those trees which you cultivate
> follow their short-lived master save
> the hated cypresses: a worthier heir
> will consume your Caecuban preserved with
> a hundred keys and will stain the pave-
> ment with its proud vintage, superior to
> that of the priests at their banquets.

"The years flow by until they are swallowed up by the
streams of the Styx and the Cocytus," comments Commager.[6]
We may add that on the sexual-symbolic level the figure
of Cocytus' sluggish stream ($\underline{1}$. 16) soon links with that
of the tree of death, the cypress, ($\underline{1}$. 23) to mark a
gloomy end to love. Nor is Horace's summons to love
while time permits (21f.) markedly more cheerful. First,
we must note that it is communicated entirely in symbolic terms. Wine (remembering Leuconoe and Lyde) and
tree combine to suggest the possibility of love, and
the fact that these must necessarily be left behind in-
sinuates that they--and, hence, love--must be exploited
now. But there is scant consolation here. The cypress
yet stands in the pleasure park; and desperation em-
bitters the drinking cup. Remarkably, Horace chooses
the carpe diem form to teach the final futility of
human pleasures.

The intricate and critical Tyrrhena regum progenies
(3:29), on the other hand, the last ode save the epilogue of the original edition, sets itself the improb-
able task of weaving a carpe diem argument that makes
no point at all of death's inevitability. Even the
correlative theme of life's brevity receives meagre notice. The result is a sparkling tour de force which
manages to offer--what was doubtless a leading motive in

its composition--the fullest statement anywhere of the
poet's hedonistic ethics.

Despite its departure from the potent formulas of
the Dellius and Hirpinus odes, this lyric is very much
an extension of those works. Aequam memento mentem
servare, Horace had warned Dellius. Here he fleshes
out his meaning. Hirpinus he had forbidden to indulge
anxiety, since life's demands are so few. This thought
is the lifeblood of the Maecenas ode. What is more,
the effects of fortune, which, as we have seen, subtly
inform those works, flowers here into the ode's most
enterprising topic. It is, in fact, the poem's extended
disquisition on fortune (33-64) which displaces the
reflections on mortality in the usual carpe diem format,
and, since it is here that the ode's ethical interest
also takes shape, it is precisely here that the ode must
prove itself technically or else quite fail.

Horace starts by inviting Maecenas to a modest
banquet at his Sabine farm. Make haste, he commands
(5ff.), and act at last on your long-harbored desire:
desert the luxury and wealth of Rome (9ff.), for simple
feasting at a poor man's board has often soothed the
cares of the great (13ff.). In terms of the work's
thematic structure, the seemingly subordinate play in
lines 9-16 on the grand over and against the simple life
easily proves the key substance of the first four
stanzas.

Now the dog days are upon us, Horace continues
(17ff.). Now the shepherd seeks shady thicket and
stream (21ff.). But you, Maecenas, fret over the common-
weal and political uncertainties at the ends of the earth
(25ff.). Yet, a wise god hides the future in darkness

and laughs if mortals are anxious beyond due measure
(29ff.).

Clearly, we are now back in the Hirpinus ode, and
a moment later, at the poem's precise center, we fetch
up in the Dellius ode: *Quod* *adest* *memento* *componere*
aequus (32f.). With Hirpinus, however, Horace had
urged an attitude of aloofness, because, in the long
run, death is all that matters. Here he takes the
shorter view and, in a demonstration of practical ethics,
contrives to show over the balance of the poem how best
to ride the crests and troughs of fortune.

Remember, set today's affairs calmly in order, the
poet advises, for the future flows like a river, now
keeping gently to its channel, now churning up horren-
dous disaster in mad deluge (33-41). Self-possessed
and happy is he who can say: I have lived, come what
may; nothing can nullify the past or undo what the
fleeting hour once has brought (41-48).

So far, a virtuoso piece, skillfully twining variegated thoughts around a central admonition to live real-
istically for today. So it will remain, but at this
point Horace himself enters the proceedings amid subtle
shocks and reverberations. Already over the course of
several stanzas the poem has been quietly forgetting,
so to speak, that its focus is Maecenas--Maecenas, whom
it grandiloquently hails in its first accents as "Scion
of Etruscan monarchs." Now, without the least shame,
it will close with Horace posturing at stage center and
Etruria's royal seed quite lost amid the properties.
Given the ode's position, this is perhaps not totally
surprising. It is time for Horace to come forward and
make his farewells. Also, his self-emphasis has its

structural function, for with the shift of focus from
the lordly Maecenas the ode turns from the grand to the
simple, an opposition which, as I have suggested, is
crucial to its thematic weave. Still, none of this alters the airy impudence with which the shift is made.
It is our first hint that humor too must be counted
among the poem's formative factors.

Fortune, rejoicing in its cruel sport, visits its
capricious blessings now upon me, avows the poet (49ff.),
now upon another. I praise her while she stays, but if
she spreads her swift wings, resigning all her gifts, I
cloak myself in my virtue and woo an honest poverty
without marriage portion (52ff.).

Horace thus prosecutes his grandeur-simplicity
theme. Extravagant good fortune is expendable; the
pauper's portion suffices. It is critical to note, however, that he does not eschew good fortune categorically.
The poem is therefore not "about" the superiority of the
simple life. Its dominant theme remains living for today, with the proviso now added that one be ever on the
ready to renounce the superfluities of sheer good luck
where occasion demands. The stress on Horace's virtue
is meant, of course, mainly for a smile, perhaps an
Epicurean smile at the Stoic's expense. But, no matter;
its true function is to pave the way for the blithe
solemnities of the last two stanzas (57ff.):

> Non est meum, si mugiat Africis
> malus procellis, ad miseras preces
>   decurrere et votis pacisci
>   ne Cypriae Tyriaeque merces
>
> addant avaro divitias mari.
> Tunc me biremis praesidio scaphae

> tutum per Aegaeos tumultus
> aura feret geminusque Pollux.

> It is not my way, if my mast groans
> beneath African blasts to have recourse
> to grovelling prayer and to strike up a
> bargain of vows lest my wares of Cyprus
> and Tyre add riches to the greedy sea.
> At that juncture, the breeze and Pollux
> the Twin will bear me safely through the
> Aegean tumult in the bulwark of my two-
> oared skiff.

We may thank Zinn for reinstating Dacier's lucid reading of the passage. In the main, Horace is simply duplicating what he has just said. When fortune turns, he will readily abandon the luxury-laden merchantman, that is, wealth itself, for a Rettungsboat, which in its turn readily corresponds to the sufficient poverty he has just "wedded".[7]

So understood, the metaphor clearly enhances the poem's ethical argument. Up to this point, Horace has dealt only with the issue of how the hedonist is to survive the loss of fortune's best favors. Now he turns to survival in the very jaws of calamity: when catastrophe strikes (not merely ship and cargo, but the poet's very life is at stake), Horace's contentment with little (the modest skiff) will preserve him from harm.

So much (this side of the symbolism) for the metaphor's content. On the formal side, we may note that it keeps a steady tenor with the imagery hitherto, first, in that it continues the play on the grand and the small and, second, in that the convulsions of fortune continue to be configured in the actions of water. But what are we to say of the miraculous aura? May we simply ascribe it to Pollux? May we even, with Pöschl, surmise that Horace's virtus (1. 55) wins him this divine grace?[8] I think not. Certain strains on the metaphor indicate that, as with the claim to virtue a moment ago, the poet is very much at play. First, if aura why tumultus? And how can a light breeze properly "carry" a lifeboat through raging seas? If, then, Pollux is the author of the aura, what service has he rendered the embattled poet? In short, the citation of the god as much heightens as explains the wonder of it all. We shall see that it takes a symbolic reading to set matters straight.

The sense of fun that, on the literal plane, glimmers only in the second half of the ode is pervasive on the symbolic level. We start, in fact, on a broad note of ribald humor, the offer of pure wine non ante verso . . . cado, "from a never upturned cask"--the playful offer, that is, of the virgo intacta. Then (6f.) the insistence that Maecenas not continue merely to contemplate "watered Tibur and the sloping plowland of Praeneste and the peaks of [Tusculum]," the female symbolized, is a suggestion that he act at last on his subliminal yearnings.[9]

A corroboratory appeal to the flesh comes with the announcement that Andromeda's resplendent father now (iam) shows his occultum ignem. Why not resplendent Maecenas, the verses hint. Then a delicate bit of counterpoint. The sense of blazing passion here, reinforced by furit and vesani in the next line, yields to an atmosphere of stunned tranquillity (21ff.):

> Iam pastor umbras cum grege languido
> rivumque fessus quaerit et horridi

81

> dumeta Silvani, caretque
> ripa vagis taciturna ventis.

> Now the shepherd with his weary
> flocks makes for the riverside, exhausted,
> and the thickets of shaggy Silvanus; and
> the quiet bank lacks wayward winds.

The figurative meaning of a thicket-fringed river needs no clarification. Meanwhile, the dearth of "wandering winds" amounts to the absence of the _aurae fallacis_ familiar from the Pyrrha ode. By suggestion, that is, the women are now docile and content. Hence, now (_iam_, l. 17; _iam_, l. 21) is the time to tend to desire, a tacit argument which is soon firmly emphasized by the axial injunction to tend to the here and now (32f.): _quod adest memento componere aequus._

Here, together with the poem itself, Horace's symbolic techniques take a fresh turn. Along with the poet, the goddess Fortuna becomes a main player over the balance of the ode, offering our poet-protagonist constant challenge through her faculty to confer benefit or harm. Her strength is in her caprice. It is the effect of the symbolism to charge this quality with the full force of female sexuality, so that both in her power to ruin and to bless the goddess becomes much the same paragon of the _sexually_ capricious female that Pyrrha represents at the beginning of the _Odes_. The only significant imagistic difference between the two is that Fortuna figures both as river and sea, while Pyrrha remains uniquely and always the sea.

Fortune, says the poet, is like a river, which sometimes glides peacefully along its channel to the

sea, but, sometimes, stirred to flood, rages wantonly,
sweeping along with it (among other things) "uprooted
trees . . . amidst the clamor of neighboring forests"
(37ff.). Symbolically, then, water, the feminine element, has the power, and without warning, to emasculate.
Plainly the passage's more literal import is not diluted
by such an intimation.

This covert play on the man-woman relationship
presently becomes open. First, as dispenser of blessings, Fortuna acquires virtual human form, especially
in the phrase ludum insolentem ludere pertinax (1. 50).
Then, completing the process, Horace deals with her no
differently than if she were one of his most prized
inamorate and poverty his plainest (53ff.). The imagery
speaks directly of wooing, of marriage, of losing the
favors of one woman and settling for those of another
distinctly less favored.

Hence, symbolically and otherwise, Horace has been
playing on the sexual power of the female for several
stanzas before he heads into the final pair. It must
also be plain that, with the closing image of escape
from a raging sea, the poem makes fast its ties with the
Pyrrha ode. The Lyde ode, which falls just before this
one, displays, we will recall, an intrinsic relation of
its own to the same lyric. Here at the close of the
Odes, in short, Horace is intent not only on linking
ending with beginning, but on staging a sexual-symbolic
reprise. Thus, for both internal and external reasons,
the passage's erotic content is critically important.
What is that content?

The sea being what it is symbolically--the female
(here fortune-as-female) in her sexuality--the ship or

boat must certainly indicate the phallus. As usual,
meanwhile, wind will signify the passions. With these
associations in mind, let us revisit the passage: best
of all is to captain the grand ship loaded with wares
of Cyprus (Aphroditic all, we note) and Tyre and sailing kindly seas; but if the sea turns vicious, Horace
will not panic; for, whatever else is taken, he can always resume his own humblest of barks, which modulated
desire (intimated by the petite craft itself, but even
more so by aura) will see through the wildest flood.
And does his escape from Pyrrha not tend to verify his
claim?

We need trouble ourselves no longer about the
passage's strained metaphor, for, plainly, not it, but
a fine symbolic tissue extending from the very start of
the Odes stands as the actual poetic matrix of these
final verses. More than that, the symbolism consoli-
dates the thematic meaning of survival through sufficient poverty by investing it with an adequately integrated form. The lightness so introduced wants apology
even less than it does explanation. Where if not in a
summons to pleasure would we expect to find our poet
non praeter solitum leves (1:6, 20)? And where if not
in his farewell ode?

So ends the main body of the primary edition.
Death's cosmic imperative is treated to a proper Horatian nose-thumbing and, in the process, the pathetic
measures of the Postumus ode all but fade from memory.

That this manifest declaration for life over death
was Horace's fundamental intention in the edition at
large is proved where proof is most telling. At the
edition's midpoint Horace collocates a subtly matched

pair of lyrics. Septimius Gadis (2:6) finds the poet
tranquilly ordering his tomb. He asks to be laid to
rest either at Tibor or Tarentum and, if at the latter,
he requests that Septimius "shed due tears on the ashes
of your poet friend while they still glow (22ff.)."
Neither here nor anywhere else in the ode is there the
least trace of a quarrel with mortality. Rather, a
serene acceptance of death's place in the sum of things
shines through. Speaking of Tarentum, Horace declares,
"For me, that corner of the world smiles beyond all
others (13f.)," and he presses the point home with a
description of the locale's perennial mildness (17ff.).
So, we surmise, will it continue to smile long after he
is dust and ashes. We are miles from the bleak resignation of the Postumus ode.

O saepe mecum (2:7) opens the gap even further.
Here Horace celebrates the restoration of Pompeius, his
comrade at Philippi, to his company after years of
separation. The opening quietly forges a close bond
with Septimi Gadis:

> O saepe mecum tempus in ultimum
> deducte Bruto militiae duce . . .

> O often brought with me to the
> supreme hour under Brutus' command . . .

Septimius too had just accompanied Horace tempus in
ultimum. But, whereas that ode spoke of death, this
sings of restoration; and if that leaves the poet a
heap of smoldering ashes, this finds him supremely
alive. Accordingly, if Mercury delivered our poet

wondrously from death at Philippi (13f.), this merely
points up the feat that he performs upon himself in the
thematic sequence between the two odes. The lyric
ends--and the second half of the collection begins--
with the start of a joyous celebration. In a word,
life conquers handsomely over death at the core of the
primary edition.

Not so in the later lyrics. The fourth book offers
two pieces in the carpe diem mould, both steeped in a
resignation to match the dolours of the Postumus ode.
The last of them, the controversial invitation to Vergil, is so bound up with 1:3 that proper treatment must
be postponed to a more convenient place. Fortunately,
however, it is also sufficiently allied to Diffugere
nives, its thematic companion piece, that conclusions
which attach to the one will also bear on the other.

If anything Diffugere nives (4:7) reneges on the
carpe diem argument more fundamentally than does Eheu
fugaces. It starts out on a series of images which,
instantly recalling the Sestius ode, raises the expectation that it likewise will be resolved in an urgent
summons to love:

Diffugere nives, redeunt iam gramina campis
        arboribusque comae;
mutat terra vices et decrescentia ripas
        flumina praetereunt;

Gratia cum Nymphis geminisque sororibus audet
        ducere nuda choros.

The snows have fled and now grasses
return to the fields and leaves to the
trees; the earth changes its season and,

subsiding, the rivers glide within
their channels; the Grace with the
Nymphs and her twin sisters dares
to disrobe and lead the choral dance.

On the symbolic level, phallic, greening trees are set
between feminine images of earth and water, themselves
respectively suggesting motions of rising and falling,
all of which lends conviction to the dance of love that
follows. But let us see what has become of love's
promise at the ode's close. Neither his lineage, eloquence nor piety will restore Torquatus once he is dead,
the poet warns, and he adds (25ff.):

> . . . infernis neque enim tenebris Diana pudicum
>   liberat Hippolytum,
> nec Lethaea valet Theseus abrumpere caro
>   vincula Perithoo.

> . . . for Diana does not free chaste
> Hippolytus from infernal darkness, nor can
> Theseus tear the Lethean chains from his be-
> loved Perithous.

Even the most exquisite affection, whether sacred or
profane, has its absolute limits. Omnia vincit mors.
    Commager convincingly demonstrates that this is
the poem's burden, and he also discloses its central
mechanism.[10] The advent of spring is meant only to pre-
sage, where mortals are concerned, the sovereignty of
winter, for, whereas nature can repair her losses, no
human can survive the winter of life's brief cycle
(13ff.). It is this thought that gives rise to the
poem's feeble carpe diem protreptic (17ff.):

> Quis scit an adiciant hodiernae crastina summae
>   tempora di superi?
> Cuncta manus avidas fugient heredis, amico
>   quae dederis animo.

> Who knows whether the gods will add to-
> morrow's hours to today's sum? Everything you
> give to your own dear soul will escape your
> heir's grasping hands.

"The vision of why it is necessary to pluck the day
seems to have paralyzed [Horace's] will to do so," comments Commager.[11] Just as this is, it misses a deeper
pathos.

Seeing that it constitutes the passage's only
reference to the affections, amico animo demands especial care. Were it not for the despondent view of love
that pervades the poem, we might limit its meaning to
the dry insinuation that no one's heir loves him as well
as he does himself. But, as we have seen, the ode
broods over a cosmic indifference to the individual that
love is pitifully helpless to affect. Given such isolation, amico animo turns love not only inward, but so far
inward as to impart that, in the end, we love and are
loved by only ourselves. Horatian counsels of mortality
have never proceeded so far.

Hence, the near abandonment of the carpe diem argument evident in the Postumus ode here verges even closer
upon realization. Add that Iam veris comites, the remaining carpe diem ode, scarcely lightens the gloom,
and we may conclude that the darker coloration already
discovered in the later love odes is nothing idiosyn-
cratic. The Horace of the fourth book is oppressed
with the thought of mortality. The full force of this

disposition does not come home to us, however, until we
become aware that, with the addition of the fifteen
lyrics of Book IV, the Postumus ode becomes the cynosure
of the entire collection.

Since it is unthinkable that Horace intended anything other than this explicit result, we must assess it
first as a piece of artistic strategy. Its one obvious
virtue on this side is also its clearest fault. By
minimal means, it achieves the fullest representation
possible of the fourth book's tenebrous genius within
the work as a whole. But that effect, though technically admirable, is also poetically distorting. For,
the fact that the funereal resignation of the Postumus
ode fails to epitomize the lyrics at large is made
acutely obvious by the affirmation of the opposite principle at the heart of the primary edition.

The fact is that we hear two lyric voices in the
Odes, the one reaching us from life's ascending curve,
the other from its descent to darkness. For Horace,
one's personal lingering beneath the sun was the only
reality. He could no more escape sorrow once he had
turned life's corner than he could court it earlier on.
Still, this is merely to say that the two strains of
his lyrics ultimately cohere. Both are functions of an
unmitigated devotion to the self. The irreducible
shade of difference is that, with time, such a commitment to life became a fear of death.

CHAPTER FOUR
MORE EROTIC ODES

In this Chapter I collect the remaining odes of
significant erotic interest where symbolism plays an
expressive part. As before, the love theme will not
always appear on the literal level, and the reader will
stand forewarned that, where, as I shall maintain, the
eroticism is essentially symbolic, we shall be entering
the most controversial waters yet. We shall begin,
however, with several lyrics where the theme is plainly
in evidence.

Horace so plots two of his symposiac odes, _Natis
in usum_ (1:27) and _Quantum distet_ (3:19), that they
form a sort of matching pair. Acting as protagonist in
both pieces, he attempts to tone down a riotous drinking party in the first, while, in the other, he goads a
set of soporific thinkers into a show of life. So far,
similitude by antithesis, but the most charming aspect
of our diptych is that both audiences are finally made
to focus on the self-same topic. Thoughts of love, our
poet seems to say, can invariably be trusted to gather
convivial wits.

Horace has just entered a drinking party in _Natis
in usum_, only to find the _bon vivants_ there assembled
hurling winecups and (as he would have us believe)

90

flashing daggers. After he manages by means of some
high sermonizing to calm the tumult (1-8), he offers to
join in the drinking on the strict condition that a
puer in attendance disclose the name of his beloved.
This is sheer badinage, of course, calculated to ease
the proceedings into gentler spheres. But the real fun
of the ode is that Horace chooses entirely the wrong
target, so that the tranquillity he wins by calming
Bacchus is lost to an unexpectedly virulent Venus.

Symbolically, through the very images of cup (its
concavity betokening the female) and dagger, which
spell riot on the literal level, the implication of
sexual violence is established early. And it is subtly
sustained throughout. The boy must confess, quo beatus
vulnere, qua pereat sagitta, violent images both. When
he hesitates, Horace pleads, "Surely whatever Venus
burns you, the fires are not shameful, and your sexual
errors are always pure-hearted." Even here, though the
intention is merely to elicit a Venus verecunda to
match the verecundus Bacchus (1. 3) already established,
the imagery is tinged with violence.

Emboldened, the lad whispers a name. "Oh, you poor
wretch," Horace cries,

> . . . quanta laborabas Charybdi
> digne puer meliore flamma.

> . . . in what a Charybdis you
> were struggling all this time, a
> boy worthy of a better flame.

Whatever the youth's specific troubles, it is clear that
Horace characterizes them by a symbol which signifies

absorbtion into the vagina. Little wonder that he ends
by declaring the unfortunate fellow all but lost beyond
redemption; but so too is his project to regulate
passion.

Quantum distet (3:19) finds Horace bored to exas-
peration by a party of companions which has gotten
bogged down in, of all things, a learned dispute on
chronology (1-4). With relentless implications that
only the present moment counts (this might indeed be
classed with the carpe diem poems), he calls in turn
for wine (5-18), song (18-20) and woman (25-28). So far
opposite the bias of 1:27 does this ode run that, after
demanding a very considerable portion of wine, the poet
exclaims, Iuvat insanire (1. 18). At least where he is
personally concerned, Bacchus verecundus is not invited.

It is no accident that in the like-numbered ode of
Book I, where it is, as here, love for Glycera that
burns him, the poet likewise calls for an abundance of
wine. Indeed, our poem's major point depends on our
seeing the Glycera both of yesterday and today. Here
is the ending (25ff.):

> Spissa te nitidum coma
>   puro te similem, Telephe, Vespero,
> tempestiva petit Rhode:
>   me lentus Glycerae torret amor meae.

> Ripe Rhode longs for you, Telephus,
> your thick hair glistening, for you, who
> resemble the clear evening star; a last-
> ing love for my Glycera burns me.

"Slow, lingering, like a smoldering fire," is Bennett's
comment on lentus. The evocation of the past caps a

pretty irony. Telephus, though he is the object of
"ripe" Rhode's instant affections, squanders his
thoughts on chronology. Horace, though his love has a
chronology of its own, burns this very moment for
Glycera. He thus draws for the abstracted gathering
the unique relevance of history to matters at hand.

The symbolic content, though fleeting, is rich.
Between his exclamation, iuvat insanire, and his explicit reference to love, the poet demands (18ff.):

> Cur Bercyntiae
> cessant flamina tibiae?
> Cur pendet tacita fistula cum lyra?

> Why no blasts of the Bercyntian
> flute? Why does the pipe hang idle,
> together with the silent lyre?

In keeping with his wish to run amok, Horace requests
not merely music, but, the Berecyntian flute being a
ritualistic instrument of the cult of Cybele, orgiastic
music. An explicit link between music and emotional
abandonment--or, better, between the absence of either--
is thus established. Specifically, though, it is
flamina that are absent. On any level the word suggests inspiration--on not the least, through wind-
symbolism, sexual inspiration. As for the flute's evident phallicism, this is turned to account in the
following line, where the implication of the pipe which
"hangs idly" derides as it laments the atmosphere
attendant on rapt scholarly discussion. Finally, the
lyre, given its hollow sounding chamber, symbolically
betokens the female and, in its complementary silence,
rounds off the suggestion of a totally absent Venus.

It is, of course, to fill this void that Rhode and
Glycera are next invoked.

The scene of _Et ture et fidibus_ (1:36) is again a
drinking party, this one, however, celebrating a specific joyous occasion, Numida's homecoming from Spain.
The poem's execution turns on a change of focal center.
In the first half, Numida's intimacy with Lamia, his
fond boyhood companion, provides the main interest.
Then, as if in passing reference, Damalis is cited as a
formidable toper (_l_. 13). But behind this hint of
sensuality lies a talent for venery which destines her
to the center of universal attention. Envisioning a
later stage of the party, the poet predicts (17ff.):

> Omnes in Damalis putris
>   deponent oculos, nec Damalis novo
> divelletur adultero
>   lascivis hederis ambitiosior.

> All will fix their languishing
> eyes on Damalis, but Damalis, more
> encompassing than wanton ivy, will
> not be torn from her new seducer.

The "new seducer" is, of course, Numida, and the portrait of the girl's drunken desire could not be more
limpid. Still, a palpably deeper understanding dawns
with the realization that at the heart of the metaphor,
twined in the web of Bacchic ivy that Damalis outweaves,
stands--the tree.

Mercuri nam te (3:11) is one of Horace's paler
love odes. Though his anxiety to attract Lyde's interest is his motive for composing it, he grants the lady
only indirect attention as he concentrates his energies

on a eulogy of music (1-24) and a recitation in epic
tones of Hypermnestra's mercy (37-52). The whole is
strung together artfully enough. Music it is which
will get the skittish Lyde to stand still and listen,
while the song, Hypermnestra's tale, will teach her to
be indulgent of her lover. Still, the poem's only link
with the finest in the love lyrics lies in its antici-
pation of the great Lyde ode (3:28) to come. It is not
till then that the theme of music's erotic efficacy,
here merely rehearsed, comes to life; and much the same
may be said of the pairing of night and Venus which
closes either ode.

The poem offers a significant piece of symbolism,
however. In the midst of his praise of the lyre, Horace remarks (15f.):

> Tu potes tigris comitesque silvas
> ducere et rivos celeres morari . . .

> You can lead tigers and woods in
> your train and slow swift rivers . . .

Though the poem's premise is that music has power to
direct the course of love, it is only here, on the symbolic level, that that key proposition is articulated.

Impios parrae (3:27), the second longest ode of
the collection, has been generally considered badly dis-
organized. It is also, in the view of Wilamowitz,
totally tasteless and absurd. This, if indefensible,
is not surprising. The poem is indeed incoherent on the
literal plane and perhaps falls short of ample resolution on any level. Also, Horace is unquestionably bold
where standards of taste are concerned. Still, once

95

allowed to go its figurative way, the lyric earns a
place among the most brilliant and fascinating in the
corpus.

Despite two eminent pieces of evidence, only
Quinn has been moved to consider the piece a love ode.[1]
First, the poem is a propempticon, a genre which, on
the authority of Menander, a rhetorician of the third
century A.D., is usually erotic in nature. Second, it
is addressed to a lady of Greek name; and how many so
aimed are not among the love odes?

Already a thread of unity begins to appear. Horace, obliged to relinquish Galatea, a girl he has
loved, to a new paramour, warns her through the example
of Europa of the possibility of dangers that lie ahead.
So far Quinn, but henceforth I must diverge from his
interpretation. Together with Williams and Friedrich,[2]
Quinn assumes that Europa has already lost her virginity
to her bull-lover at the time she delivers her long complaint (34-76). Seeing that she is therefore already
abandoned, her straits serve as a warning to Galatea of
a like fate at the hands of her new lover. This,
though appealingly tidy, simply does not conform to the
evidence of the poem. First of all, Horace tells us
that Europa delivers her lament as soon as she reaches
Crete (simul . . . tetigit, l. 33). The bull therefore
must necessarily have consummated his design en route.
How, understandably, Quinn does not explain. Second,
Quinn's position leads him to shirk a long-standing
challenge of the commentators: if the Europa story is
meant as a caveat to Galatea, how do we explain its
happy ending? Our task, then, is to test whether the
tale makes sense as cautionary erotic advice despite

its ending and without presumption of a post-coital
abandonment. We shall find, I think, that it does, but
only if we penetrate to the ode's subtlest psychological
and symbolic levels.

After calling down foul omens upon all scoundrels
(Impios, l. 1) in their travels and promising, as a
"prophetic augur" (l. 8), fair ones to those he cher-
ishes, Horace promptly assures Galatea that she enjoys
all the benefits of the latter class (13ff.):

> Sis licet felix, ubicumque mavis,
> et memor nostri, Galatea, vivas,
> teque nec laevus vetet ire picus
>   nec vaga cornix.

> May you be happy wherever you
> please to be, and may you live remem-
> bering me, and may neither the ill-
> omened woodpecker nor the vagrant
> crow thwart your progress.

Again, we hypothesize with Quinn that the poet here
magnanimously bestows his blessing on Galatea as she
abandons him for some indeterminate romantic adventure.

But just as Horace's claim to prophecy is tentative at best, so, it seems, is his display of genero-
sity, for, with a sudden access of anxiety, he subjoins
(17ff.):

> Sed vides quanto trepidet tumultu
> pronus Orion. Ego quid sit ater
> Hadriae novi sinus et quid albus
>   peccet Iapyx.

> Hostium uxores puerique caecos
> sentiant motus orientis Austri et

> aequoris nigri fremitum et trementis
>   verbere ripas.

> But you see how thunderously Orion
> rages as he sinks. I know what the
> black gulf of the Adriatic can be and
> how deceitful is the clear Iapygian wind.
> May the wives and children of enemies ex-
> perience the blind rush of the gathering
> south wind and the shores shuddering be-
> neath its blow [rather than you].

First, a key question. Are we to infer a literal sea-
journey to the east and nothing more? The evidence is
better that the voyage is wholly figurative. Commenting on what he regards the poem's loose organization,
Fraenkel remarks that, though Horace's warning to
Galatea reduces itself to "beware the storm", the
Europa episode contains no mention of foul weather
whatsoever.[3] But Horace was not so inept. The storm
that Europa experiences is, of course, figurative,
consisting of the psychological tumult which the poet
soon places plainly in evidence. If, then, Horace does
not intend a literal storm, how can we insist on a
literal voyage? Even if we do, we must concede that
the implicit meaning of the passage takes precedence
over such mere data. And the implicit meaning is
charged with symbolism. The ship which will transport
Galatea suggests the phallus and the sea the vagina.
This further discloses the nature of her new enterprise,
while, at the least, the symbolism of the brewing storm
implies dire psychological peril.
  The upshot is that Horace is now attempting to
thwart Galatea's departure as earnestly as he had

earlier encouraged it. Which of these two attitudes is the more genuine does not come clear till the poem's end.

The Europa story constitutes the balance of the ode. Because critics have in the main assumed the telling of this tale to be Horace's only real motive in composing the ode, the prime interpretive question has gone begging. Why Europa? Why, that is, this particular story to throw light on Galatea's circumstances? No analysis so framed could fail to uncover the vital link of sexuality.

Meanwhile, the very transition to the Europa episode promotes the hypothesis of an erotic unity (25ff.):

> Sic et Europa niveum doloso
> credidit tauro latus et scatentem
> beluis pontum mediasque fraudes
>   palluit audax.

>   Just so did Europa entrust her
> snowy flank to the crafty bull and
> pale, for all her courage, at the sea '
> teeming with beasts and the dangers
> all around her.

If Galatea is misplacing her trust in the ship just as Europa did hers in the bull, the evident phallic implication of the former is greatly reinforced, which, in turn, enhances the sense of an erotic linkage between the two episodes.

Who on first acquaintance with the myth of Europa has failed to wonder how such a relationship can come to be? Horace minces no words on the reason (1. 47): the girl felt enormously attracted to the beast. Surely an

99

innocent attraction? He does not encourage that conclusion. The only aspect of guilt that greatly interests him, however, is Europa's reluctance to accept her
sexuality, dark and monstrous though it may be, for
what it is. Thus, the main thrust of his presentation
is to lay bare the futility of her self-evasion.

Horace sets the psychological groundwork for the
entire passage with the verses of transition that we
have already seen. Europa's hallucinatory vision of
sea-beasts at this juncture is obviously to be explained
as a reflex of fear. But what is it that she fears?
The brute that swims beneath her, for one. Yet, only
moments earlier she had been powerfully drawn to this
creature. Her shock and terror must thus also involve
the attraction itself. Horace's familiar sea-symbolism
supports this conjecture. According to its usual application, the sea represents female sexuality, in this
case, Europa's own. From one perspective, therefore,
the bull's unceremonious plunge therein bears its own
diaphanous meaning. More pertinent to our present
thought, however, is the inference that the swarming
beasts that Europa beholds represent the demons of her
own sexuality--a collective representation, when all is
said, of the brutish passion that brought her here in
the first place. She is mortified because she now beholds them in vera re for the first time. If repression
is the result, this merely tells us how much Horace knew
of "modern" psychology.

Horace reserves one further word of introduction,
at first glance a wistful reflection on lost innocence:
she who was so recently (nuper, l. 29) weaving garlands
for the nymphs now "in the glimmering night sees nothing

but stars and waves." But is the weaving of garlands
for the nymphs--themselves the embodiment of the sea's
eroticism--all that innocent an activity? And is
Europa really out of her element? If the sea represents her sexuality, then to be transported as she now
has been into its nocturnal expanse is to be ushered
into her own secret element and nature, the fruition of
a desire of which flower-plaiting in the nymphs' honor
is a sheer sublimation. In short, Europa was overripe
for sexual experience, her innocence reduced to precisely that impulsive trust which raised her to the
back of the beauteous bull.

Though suppressing her real desire for the bull,
she does not herself pretend to innocence. Rather, she
cannot believe the sordidness of her circumstances.
Her abandonment of home and hearth, she laments, has de-
prived her of the right to the name of daughter and of
all claim to goodness (34ff.). Death itself, she
suggests, would be too slight a punishment for her
villainy (37f.). Hence, her self-contempt is utterly
plain. What, then, does she have to say of the bull?
Everything, as it turns out, that she means to conceal
(45ff.):

> Si quis infamem mihi nunc iuvencum
> dedat iratae, lacerare ferro et
> frangere enitar modo multum amati
>   cornua monstri.
>
>   . . . O deorum
> si quis haec audis, utinam inter errem
>   nuda leones!
>
> Antequam turpis macies decentis
> occupet malas teneraeque sucus

101

> defluat praedae, speciosa quaero
> pascere tigres.

> If now in my fury someone should
> put that vile bullock in my power, I
> would try to maim it with steel and
> shatter its horns, for all that I loved
> it greatly a while ago. . . . Oh if any
> of you gods hear my words, let me wander
> naked among lions! Before ugly wasting
> fastens upon my lovely cheeks and the
> tender juices dry in their prey, I wish
> in the fullness of my beauty to become
> food for tigers.

These lurid cravings to fall victim to other and wilder beasts surely betray that, where our simple bull is concerned, the lady protests much too much.

Even the advice she next offers herself in her father's name secretly articulates her unresolved desires (57ff.): she can either hang herself from a nearby ash tree or, committing herself to the "swift winds", plunge to the rocks below. Only allow voice to the symbolism of tree and wind and the punishment for her guilty desires becomes their spectral enactment.

The mortified girl's last words (63ff.) touch emphatically upon her prime concern, her regal dignity. She contemplates suicide because, marooned as she is, the only alternative she can see is to become bedmate to a barbarian and slave to his wife. This degrading outcome her pride must reject--precisely as it has the sordid facts of her sexuality.[4]

Venus, who quite understands all of this, now suddenly materializes together with Cupid. Nothing in their manner suggests that they anticipate the least

trouble with Europa. While Venus greets the girl with
mocking laughter, Cupid stands by with bow unstrung.
The task of enflaming Europa, that is, is well completed.
Venus adds an ironic word, however (69ff.):

> Mox ubi lusit satis, 'Abstineto'
> dixit 'irarum callidae rixae,
> cum tibi invisus laceranda reddat
>   cornua taurus . . . '

>   Then, when she had sported enough,
> she said, "Be prepared to quit your an-
> ger and hot complaints when the loath-
> some bull serves up his horns for you
> to shatter . . . "[5]

Can this presentation of the horns mean anything other
than what it cries out to say symbolically? Europa's
fantastic desire, reaffirmed a moment ago by the very
manner of its denial, is thus on the point of being
fulfilled. It remains only to supply a happy ending,
which Horace happily does. Europa (says Venus) must
learn to endure her great fortune of being the bride of
Jupiter: half the world will bear her name.

   Now as to Galatea. It is easy enough to see how
the Europa story warns of compromising perils that may
lie ahead--not the least, perils springing from still
unsorted emotions. But what of the happy ending? Its
difficulty lies not, as the commentators have felt, in
its happiness, but in the superfluous wealth of its detail. In particular, the disclosure that Europa's bull
is none but Jupiter bears no significant relationship to
the "bull" that is Galatea's lover. Still, a perfectly
sound resolution results if we merely listen to the tale

with the ears for which it was intended. At first
lavish and then stinting with his blessings, Horace
has ended on a resolving note of affirmation. Can
Galatea help but conclude that his more generous nature
has won out in the end? She will meanwhile observe
that the happy ending comes only after a cruel and
desperate voyage of self-discovery.

A sea voyage is also at the heart of Quid fles
Asterie (3:7), and its symbolic implication communi-
cates a tale substantially opposite that which Horace
lavishes upon the ode's anxious heroine. Asterie's
lover, Gyges, having started upon a mercantile voyage
to Bithynia, has been driven off course to Oricum in
Epirus by a violent September storm. Horace asks
Asterie to believe that, despite the most ardent appli-
cations of a lady of that place, a wooing that enjoys
the services of a wonderfully corrupt go-between and
does not stop short of mortal threats if the youth
fails to respond, Gyges remains heroically loyal to her.

Even if the tale did not betray its own contri-
vance, the symbolism would. Gyges is driven off course
after the "mad [rising] of the constellation of the
goat (5f.)." Stormy winds tend to signify an explosion
of passion in Horace. Here their expression through
the epithet insana (1. 6)--not to mention the contribution of the goat--render the connotation even more certain than usual. And if, symbolically, the ship is
again the phallus, all hopes for Gyges' fidelity are
lost. We can appreciate that he had small choice in
the matter, storm-passions being what they are; neither
is it unreasonable that he must postpone his return
till the tempests have cleared (1. 2). But this hardly

adds up to staunch devotion.

Nor is Horace yet nearly through with his satiric posturings. There is an evident play on Odysseus' plight in Gyges' fortunes, while Asterie is a patent Penelope. How well, then, has she been fulfilling her own obligations? Not very, it seems. Her neighbor, Enipeus (Alcinous too was a neighbor), may please her more than is just (22ff.). Worse, he is by intimation sexually devastating, for he is at once a superb horseman and first among swimmers; plains and waterways, that is, feministic both in symbolic implication, are but the scenes of his conquests. "Domum claude," advises Horace with a closing symbolic flourish. How humorless that command if he has not been overstating Gyges' fidelity.

Pastor cum traheret (1:15) has won scant admiration from Horace's critics. By far the major interest it has stimulated has focused on the question of whether it might be a political allegory. Happily, that theory is in eclipse.[6] On the side of aesthetics, Nisbet and Hubbard fairly well sum up the common view by pronouncing the ode's execution "more persevering than successful." Superficially, it does seem a rather stiff effort. What is the need of a solemn prophecy of Nereus to acquaint us with the folly and cowardice of Paris? But to leave it at that is to miss at least two crucial factors. The ode's position, as we shall see, is easily as meaningful as its content. And, second, there is the symbolism.

The poem opens with Paris' fleet becalmed as he hastens homeward with his elegant prize:

> Pastor cum traheret per freta navibus
> Idaeis Helenen perfidus hospitam,

> ingrato celeris obruit otio
> ventos, ut caneret fera
>
> Nereus fata . . .

> When the faithless shepherd was
> conveying his host, Helen, over the
> seas in Idaean ships, Nereus muffled
> the swift winds with an unwelcome calm,
> so as to prophesy his dire destiny . . .

To this I would like to juxtapose the last stanza but
one, where Nereus describes the onset of Diomedes
(28ff.),

> . . . quem tu, cervus uti vallis in altera
> visum parte lupum graminis immemor,
> sublimi fugies mollis anhelitu,
> non hoc pollicitus tuae.

> . . . whom you, soft as you are,
> like a stag who has caught sight of a
> wolf on the opposite side of a valley,
> will flee, forgetting his pasturage,
> with gasping head upraised, for all
> your promises to your beloved.

The poetic correlations between these two passages are
nothing less than dazzling. Paris' amorous designs are
interrupted in both places, first by word (the prophecy),
then by deed. His response reveals a great deal, for,
later on, ironically, he displays as much eagerness to
abandon his desires as he did earlier to implement them.
This deftly takes the measure of the man, but it is the
work of the symbolism to give it eloquence. On the female side, the symbolism of the sea that opens the ode

gives way to that of the valley at the close. Meanwhile, the figure of impeded progress (the ship becalmed), which is all involuntary in the first passage,
yields to that of deliberate, indeed impotent (<u>mollis</u>,
<u>1</u>. 31), withdrawal in the second. But most striking of
all is the wind imagery in its adumbration of the
passions. The enforced smothering of passion intimated
by <u>ventos</u> <u>obruit</u> is released in the sudden gasps of
<u>sublimi</u> <u>anhelitu</u>; and the fact that such pantings mark
anything but the consummation of the love embrace for
which Paris was earlier so impatient completes the
crushing irony of the piece. Figuratively, Paris is
mockèd and demolished where he is utterly strongest.

So much for the poem's intrinsic execution. Let
us turn now to the matter of its placement. It opens,
as we have seen, with an image of sailing that encour-
ages a phallic interpretation. Immediately preceding
there occurs an ode which, being addressed directly and
most familiarly to nothing other than a ship, not merely bears but demands a symbolic construction (1:14):

> O navis, referent in mare te novi
> fluctus! O quid agis? Fortiter occupa
>   portum! Nonne vides ut
>   nudum remigio latus,
>
> et malus celeri saucius Africo
> antemnaeque gemant, ac sine funibus
>   vix durare carinae
>   possint imperiosius
>
> aequor? Non tibi sunt integra lintea,
> non di quos iterum pressa voces malo.
>   Quamvis Pontica pinus,
>   silvae filia nobilis,

iactes et genus et nomen inutile,
nil pictis timidus navita puppibus
    fidit. Tu, nisi ventis
        debes ludibrium, cave.

Nuper sollicitum quae mihi taedium,
nunc desiderium curaque non levis,
    interfusa nitentis
        vites aequora Cycladas.

      O ship, new breakers will sweep
you back to sea! Oh, what are you
doing? Make for port with all your
might! Do you not see how your side,
stripped of oarage, your mast, stricken
by the swift south wind, and your yards
all groan, how your hull, reft of stays,
can scant endure the water's overbearing force? Your sails are no longer
whole; neither are your gods, on whom
to call when you are once again whelmed
with woe. Although you are a Pontic
pine, the daughter of a noble forest,
useless is the name and lineage you may
boast of, and the sailor takes no heart
in your bright embellishments. You, I
say; unless you are destined to be a
sport of the winds, beware. You who
were lately my weary distress, but now
my yearning and heavy care, shun the
waters that flow between the shining
Cyclades.

Ever since Quintilian this troubled craft has been
equated with the ship of state. My own conviction is
that it connotes the phallus, with the poem as a whole
representing a serio-comic Horatian expostulation to
that amorously impulsive side of his own nature that we
have come to know so well. Interestingly, W. S. Anderson has anticipated this view at least to the extent of

positing an erotic context.[7] But to Anderson the ship
is a woman, a former mistress of the poet whom he is
now, out of renewed interest, desperately trying to
save from the allegorical seas of love. Seeing that
none of the three interpretations can be authenticated
on internal evidence alone, the ode's position, if it
has anything to tell us, assumes unusual significance.

In this connection we find that Pastor cum
traheret, since it opens on a phallic nautical image,
makes a harmonious sequel to O Navis if the ship there
is similarly construed. In contrast, the ship-as-woman
reading produces an abrupt symbolic reversal, while,
for its part, the ship of state bears no figurative relationship to Paris' flagship at all.

Moreover, the harmony between the two odes, pro-
viding the sailing imagery is taken as phallic, runs
quite deep. If Horace is recalling himself from an
impetuous erotic adventure in 1:14, Pastor cum traheret
serves as a felicitous mythological exemplum of the
sort of penalty that attends such recklessness. In
keeping with this, Paris is introduced in 1:15 as a
sport of the winds, the very kind of thing that Horace
warned against at the close of O navis; and, by the same
token, the truce to passion besought there is realized--
all the more pointedly for being ironic and obligatory--
at the start of 1:15. The alternative interpretations
generate no such concinnities.

The phallic interpretation of O Navis proves even
more attractive once the preceding ode, Cum tu Lydia,
is added to the balance. To appreciate this at its
best, however, we must trace the development of the love
motif since the Pyrrha ode. There Horace had encountered

109

disaster, whose setting was--most significantly for our present ode--the sea. His next overture (1:8) is a piece addressed to none else than Lydia. But his approach here is tentative, ironic, masking any thought of direct interest with a mocking concern for the welfare of Sybaris. Then (1:9, 1:11) come two carpe diem pieces, and with the second (the Leuconoe ode) the Pyrrha debacle has unmistakably begun to lose its deterrent force. But if Horace harbors a palpable yen for Leuconoe, its expression is at once light and abstract enough to stay well clear of enthrallment.

That comes with Cum tu Lydia, even if, as I have suggested, we interpret its romanticism to be cynical to the core. In that case, the fervor expressed is unquestionably reduced to sheer lust. But lust too enthralls. In spite of his better counsel, then, Horace has delivered himself up once again to the erotic wars--or, better, to its seas. It is, in fact, the experience of Pyrrha that gives point to the re- of referunt in the first line of O navis. He is being drawn back into the same devouring jaws of the sea-as-woman which he had so narrowly escaped only (so to speak) a moment past. Hence his plangent and desperate self-adjurations in O Navis to beware.

Now to the ode itself. The ship of state interpretation, though it fares tolerably well over the bulk of the poem, simply collapses in the last stanza. Not only, as Anderson advises, is the love language that suddenly blooms there unsuited to a political context, but the final couplet is even less adaptable. With all specific emphasis, Horace singles out the Cycladic waters as a particular source of menace to the ship.

But by no stretch of the imagination did they harbor danger for the dreadnought that was Rome. One notes that Nisbet and Hubbard, cleaving to the ship of state hypothesis, pronounce Anderson's a "strange theory."[8] Perhaps so; but is it any less odd to marry the concept of Augustan Rome as a witless beloved that must at all costs shun the blue Aegean?

The obvious attraction of Anderson's interpretation is that it lends instantaneous meaning to the love language. But it also entails a plague of difficulties. First, the aesthetics are dubious. The poet's renewed interest in the lady of tattered sails must be born of pity, not desire. A nice sentiment this, but not Horatian. Also, the imputation of noble lineage at 11f. compels Anderson to posit a high-born lady as the addressee; but Horace's _innamorate_ are without exception mist-shrouded Greeklings born strictly of his imagination. Worst of all, not only does Anderson's construction disturb the sequential flow of the love lyrics that we have just noted, but, surely, it needs the corroboration of an instance or two in Horace where the ship signifies the female. On both counts it is especially vulnerable in that it offers no correlation with the Pyrrha ode, where the erotic significance of sea and ship was first and formidably established. And, finally, while it is manifest why Horace might have gone to such extravagant lengths to dissimulate an address to his phallus, the motivation if his ship is merely a woman is unaccountable. Indeed, if this is its solution, the riddle seems more a trial of patience than of wit.

It remains to validate the ship's phallicism in its own right. If the opening exclamations do not put us in

mind of the Pyrrha ode, verses 3-10, with their catalo-
gue of accrued damages at sea rush to fill the void.
It was, indeed, Pyrrha who administered the mauling in
the first place. Nor does the ensuing suggestion of
nobility offer particular difficulty. We are dealing
here with the simple, universal phenomenon of phallic
pride. No less than _Pontica_--the provenance of the
ancient world's finest shiptimber--is the poet's _pinus_.
Thus, putting the seeming difficulty of _filia_ (_l_. 12)
aside for a moment, we may take verses 13-15 to declare
simply that virile vanity offers no key to the present
crisis.

A rational resolve seems to, however, at least
fleetingly. Symbolically, the winds that threaten to
make a plaything of the ship (15f.) are the same that
blew in the Pyrrha ode. Beware, Horace sensibly commands, unless you are doomed to helplessness. To my
mind one of the ode's most vital graces is its tacit
revelation that the ship is just so doomed. The brusque
tone of command in _cave_, softens to a forlorn plea with
vites, as, playing his last, desperate card, the poet
shifts his appeal from the mind to the heart (_desiderium_,
cura non levis)--and, surely, loses.

But it remains the phallus to which he symbolically
addresses himself throughout, not the least the phallus
as the wayward, irresponsible beloved. The fact that
Horace has, in effect, feminized that organ with the
description _filia_ in line 12 lends a certain verisimili-
tude to his romantic pleadings, but their real conviction takes its rise elsewhere. Nothing is needed to
explain how the phallus, which is to say Horace's erotic
impulses, might have been a "weary distress" in the

112

chaste interlude since the Pyrrha experience. Now it
has become his "yearning and heavy care" precisely because these same urges are once more escaping his control. So qualified, even the sense of separation inherent in desiderium is validated.[9] Horace is addressing a second, rampantly Dionysiac self, which is now
launched upon a course utterly its own. In view of the
peril--shipwreck, and on the symbolic level, castra-
tion--the expostulations of endearment are scarcely a
surprise.

As far as it goes, Anderson's handling of the forbidden seas "that flow between the shining Cyclades" is
unassailable. These, he argues, are the bailiwick of
Venus, hence, of love; and his citation of Venus'
presidency over the fulgentis Cycladas at 3:28, 14
places the issue beyond doubt. But this is a scant
beginning. The mention of Grecian waters naturally
puts us in mind of Horace's various Greek innamorate.
Likewise, nitentes, for the same word in its various
forms serves as a description of Glycera, Barine and,
most appositely, Pyrrha. Besides, through a graceful
instance of metonymy, it here comes to modify the sea
itself, thus precisely recollecting the radiant, perilous waters-as-woman of the Pyrrha ode. Meanwhile, the
same end is accomplished by even simpler means. Apply-
ing the root sense of Cyclades, we come up with the
reading: "Avoid the waters that flow between the shining encurvatures." The ship is no female.

Horace addressed one other ode, the propempticon
for Vergil (1:3), to a ship. This poem, by no means a
simple piece, is best understood in its relationship to
4:12, the carpe diem lyric which, as we have seen,

113

beckons Vergil to much-qualified revelry. A prior question obtrudes, however. Is the Vergil of 4:12 in fact
the famous poet? Not everyone is so persuaded:

> When we recollect the language that
> Horace used of Vergil elsewhere, the
> animae dimidium meae of 1.3.6, the
> animae quales nequae candidiores/terra
> tulit neque queis me sit devinctior
> alter of Sat. 1.5.41, the optimus
> Virgilius of Sat. 1.6.55, we shall be
> able to appreciate the taste of those
> who here consider that Horace, in a
> book published after his death, can
> speak of him as the 'client of noble
> youths' and sneeringly hint at meanness
> and fondness for money-making.

So T. E. Page.[10] Fraenkel is just as astringent:[11]

> It has not escaped my notice that from
> time to time somebody attempts once
> more to show that the addressee of this
> ode is the author of the Aeneid. Even
> if we disregard for a moment the im-
> probability of a much earlier ode being
> included in the fourth book--fancy Hor-
> ace addressing the poet Vergil of all
> men as iuvenum nobilium cliens and as-
> cribing to him studium lucri, and then
> publishing the poem after his friend's
> death! A minimum of common human feel-
> ing should save us from the sense of
> humor that turns Horace, the most tact-
> ful of poets, into a monster of human
> callousness.

Stronger strictures from sources so formidable would be
hard to come by. Still, opposition persists, notably
from Perret, Collinge, Hahn and Quinn.[12] For the most

114

part, however, these scholars do not base their arguments on the correlations between 4:12 and 1:3, which
grounds, as I hope to show, clinch the matter of identification once and for all and, into the bargain,
fashion a far more delicate and interesting problem of
interpretation than either Page or Fraenkel begin to
imagine.

We shall examine the relationship between the two
lyrics on two levels, first, the place that each holds
structurally in the Odes and, second, the interplay,
mostly thematic, between the two.

The first three odes of Book I concern, in order,
Maecenas, Augustus and Vergil. Though nothing in the
third ode makes this identification positive, incidentally, no one doubts that the poet Vergil is there
intended. Of the last five odes of the fourth book two
concern Augustus, one Maecenas and one Vergil. The remaining piece (4:13) involves one of Horace's fictive
sweethearts. We may thus say that the Odes as they
stand begin and end with eminent reference to three
historical figures who were not only giants in their
own right but bulked very large in Horace's fortunes
and affections. How reasonable is it to insist that one
of these figures, identified by name in both places, is
really intended only in one? Better, were it not even
more absurd, to maintain that he was intended in
neither instance. In any event, let us examine how
seriously even these smallest of observations affect the
position taken by Page and Fraenkel. Horace, they
would have us believe, knew an obscure businessman
named Vergil, and, honoring him with a slight and rather
curious carpe diem piece, proceeds to assign it a posi-

115

tion which must inevitably confound him with the poet
of that name and shatter the symmetry of the collection
as well. No Roman poet operates in this manner.

True, the symmetry is not impeccable. Not only
do the dignitaries addressed in the two places not
appear in the same order, but the latter ode stands
fourth from the end, one position short of perfect correspondence. Still, the shortfall is not absolute.
Iam veris comites, as well as an address to Vergil, is
the last carpe diem ode of the collection. The first
is 1:4. Both poems start with a description of spring's
advent, and both invoke--at identical stages (11f. in
each case)--the god Pan/Faunus. From the standpoint of
symmetry, therefore, 4:12 picks up both 1:3 and 1:4,
thus drawing the former more nearly into balance with
itself.

The internal evidence is even more formidable.
Sic te diva opens with a wish for Vergil's fair passage
to Attica. In the second stanza of 4:12 we are presented with (Cecropiae domus, l. 6) the same land. Then
the whole of the third stanza is strikingly reminiscent
of the Eclogues, which naturally puts us in mind of the
poet Vergil. Finally, Vergil's name surfaces immediately thereafter (l. 13). If this sequence does not
yet establish an indisputable linkage with 1:3, the sequel, I think, settles the issue decisively.

It has often been observed that the opening of 1:3
teems with commercial imagery. Vergil is creditum to
the ship that bears him off; in turn, the ship owes him
(debes, l. 6) to Horace; hence the poet's plea: reddas
incolumem. Furthermore, as Nisbet and Hubbard point
out, Horace's prayer actually constitutes a quid pro quo

116

between poet and ship: fair winds in return for a safe
passage. Quid pro quo, it hardly needs argument, is the
central notion of 4:12; if Vergil wishes to share Horace's wine, he must come with a contribution of his own
(1. 22f.), a box of nard. We are thus still in the
marketplace; and, as we shall see, the representation
of Vergil as a businessman of sorts of 4:12 must take
its explanation at least in part from this larger
commercial metaphor. But we utterly miss the point of
the quid pro quo in 4:12 if we fail to heed its ironic
relationship to the beautiful animae dimidium meae in
1:3. Vergil, who was there half of Horace's own heart,
must now earn his own way (nardo vina merebere, 1. 16)
if he is to share the other's society. He must "go
halves!" If Horace was unaware of this fine antithetical interplay, so subtle, yet so explosive, he was no
friend of the muses. Surely we must deduce that the
Vergilius of 4:12 is not only the Vergilius of 1:3, but
a Vergil represented as somehow fallen from Horace's
unqualified good graces.

Can Horace be in earnest? Further structural
probings allow a surprisingly precise answer.

We will recall that the structural center of the
first three books is occupied by a balanced pair of
lyrics (2:6 and 2:7) addressed, in order, to the poet's
intimate friends, Septimius and Pompeius. That the fact
of friendship is thematic is demonstrated not only be
the content of either ode, but by the matching construction, which gives us the word mecum (suggestive of intimacy) coupled with a vocative at the beginning of
each piece and the word amicus at the very end. It thus
begins to emerge that Horace made the intimacies of

117

amicitia a structural keynote of the primary edition of
the Odes by emphasizing them here at the center, at the
beginning with Sic te diva and at the close with the
great Maecenas ode, Tyrrhena regum progenies (3:29).

Closer examination shows abundant thematic har-
monies between 1:3 and 2:6 and 7 viewed in tandem.
First of all, a certain parallel obtains between the
principal players. Septimius is a poet, Pompeius an
adventurer, while the Vergil of 1:3 is (with, for the
moment, a bit of charity) both. Also, the "plots" are
analagous. Vergil in 1:3 is sent off on a journey, but
only amid anxious hopes for his safe restoration; while
2:6, opening on the theme of journeying and looking to
Horace's ultimate departure from life, is keyed to
leave-taking, and 2:7 centers on restoration from wan-
derings. Most interesting of all, both of the latter
odes share in the debere-reddere "commercial" imagery
of Sic te diva. Septimius must shed a tear that is
debita (2:6, 13) over the ashes of his poet friend,
while Horace urges Pompeius, obligatam redde Iovi dapem
(2:7, 17), in recognition of his safe return. The
manner in which Pompeius discharges this debt is also
instructive, for it is in fact Horace who pays it out
of his own stores (15ff.). Their separate personalities
thus tend to merge into one, which is tacitly reminiscent
of 1:3 and its animae dimidium meae. In short, both in
form and content these three odes combine into a distinct structural series centering on the partings and
reunions of fast friends and the generosities and obligations attaching thereto.

Much the same themes are articulated in the second
half of the primary edition through the medium of Hor-

ace's relationship with Maecenas. An obvious bridge
poem in this connection is Cur me querelis (2:17).
Here Horace styles Maecenas meae partem animae, thereby
picking up, in a slightly paler hue, the key endearment
of Sic te diva. Also, he rekindles the theme of intimacy unto death that informs the Septimius ode by vowing
that he could not bear to die on any other than the same
day as Maecenas (8ff.). Even the Pompeius ode's theme
of joyous restoration is revisited (22ff.), together
with a touch of the familiar "commercial" imagery (30f.),
which once more dwells on the rendering of due obligations.

Taking the Septimius ode as a point of departure,
the poem also weaves something peculiarly its own into
the thematic web of amicitia. Both odes are remarkable
for, first, an air of acceptance toward death and, also,
a profound sense of comradeship. Not surprisingly,
they complement each other on these grounds. Septimius
and Horace, as it were, journey forth together toward
the place where Horace will rest his bones forever.
Similarly, Maecenas and Horace companion each other
toward an appointed time. But this only elaborates on
a harmony already detected between the two pieces. What
is remarkably new in the Maecenas ode is its equation
of life's value with the value of friendship. Without
Maecenas, life is nothing, Horace insists. Without
Maecenas, therefore, death for Horace is nothing. There
is little that is Horatian in such a claim, to be sure,
and we may decline to believe him. Still, the theme of
amicitia touches gracious new heights.

Originally, Tyrrhena regum progenies was intended
to complete the entire thematic structure. It responds

to the Vergil ode and its theme of separation by calling
for a reunion of friends, thus recalling the Pompeius
ode as well. Imagery from commerce is also abundantly
in evidence, coming forth most clearly at the midpoint
(Quod adest memento componere aequus) and where Horace
claims to be ever prepared to write off fortune's
blessings as losses (resigno quod dedit, 1. 54). These
details, however, are only incidental to a much larger
design. The entire ode may be said to center on the
metaphor of life's proper account books with fortune.
Thus, Horace's pervasive argument for the sufficiency of
pauperhood redeems itself doubly. Most adroitly, too,
the poet's pose as a seafaring merchant in the closing
lines rounds off the commercial play that takes its
rise at the very start of Sic te diva.

Keeping in mind the genial intellectualism of this
particular ode, we may conclude that the five pieces
together place on display, besides a high order of
sustained thematic art, Epicurean friendship of the
richest refinement. How very different the final Vergil
ode with its spirit of grudging mistrust and its un-
pleasant haggling.[13] And the apparent gulf between the
two friends grows even wider in the light of a few further thematic details. At the beginning of Tyrrhena
regum progenies Horace freely offers Maecenas virgin
wine together with unguent. Similarly, to Pompeius
(2:7, 21ff.):

> Oblivioso levia Massico
> ciboria exple; funde capacibus
> unguenta de conchis.

> Fill the smooth cups with forget-
> ful Massic; pour unguents from capa-
> cious shells.

It is precisely these two items in combination that the
poet will _not_ lavish on Vergil in 4:12. Also, compare
the closes of the Pompeius and Vergil odes. Recepto/
dulce mihi furere est amico, Horace exclaims to
Pompeius; while for Vergil he has only the pallid imitation, dulce est desipere in loco. In sum, at practically every turn in 4:12 we encounter a distinct and
obviously deliberate qualification of a largesse and
enthusiasm which had come to seem only routine between
Horace and his bosom companions. We can only infer that
Vergil has somehow offended his poet friend, and that
rather severely.

Horace reserves one final, balming stroke, however.
In the last verses of the very last ode, he crowns a
eulogy of Augustus with the remark that the emperor's
gift of peace has freed him to sing of dead Roman
leaders,

> Troiamque et Anchisen et almae
> progeniem Veneris.

But this was Vergil's song, and, clearly, these verses
are Horace's tribute to Vergil--for our interests a gesture as significant as it is graceful and delicate.
Horace had ended Books II and III with tributes to his
own poetic achievements. Now, later in life, he offers
a new close, qualifying his poetry in such a way as to
compel us to think of Vergil.[14] The two being thus
identified once again as one, the equation animae

dimidium meae is tactfully restored.

To sum up. Iam veris comites, when related to the
work's key odes on the subject of amicitia discloses an
ineluctable diminution of feeling for Vergil, yet nothing, as it turns out, which hinders Horace from merg-
ing his very artistic identity with his poet friend's.
It follows that we are looking for an offense of a private nature which Horace can perhaps forgive, but never
forget. Though this leaves a wide range of possibili-
ties, we may expect that, barring a sorry collapse of
art at the last moment, the poetry will spontaneously
yield up the solution. This, as I hope to show, it
does, but not without disturbing some fundamental pre-
sumptions concerning the nature of the friendship between the two poets.

The essential flaw in the relationship comes to
light by virtue of the commercial motif. In 4:12, while
casting Vergil in the part of a merchant, Horace imputes
the charge of a studium lucri, a "penchant for profit."
We will recall that at the close of 3:29 the poet assigned himself the role of merchant, but with a signal
difference in characterization. There Horace declared
himself content with little, whereas Vergil is the
express opposite. Here is the sore spot. Such contrast-
ing natures can scarcely form harmonious halves of a
single soul.

We may further infer that Vergil's specific fault
lies in seeking and taking unfair advantage in friendship. The most striking feature of 4:12 is that Vergil
is refused unconditional hospitality. In part the explanation lies in the epithet iuvenum nobilium cliens.
Vergil, it would appear, is something of a parasite.

Even more distinctly, it attaches to the charge of
studium lucri. Surely Horace's uncharacteristic reluctance to regale a bosom friend must be connected with
Vergil's "penchant for profit," and the connection can
only be that Horace will not allow himself to be exploited. The box of nard demanded of Vergil must therefore represent an earnest of his honest intentions--
proof, in other words, that he craves Horace's affections for their own sake and not merely for their fruits.

Horace's mistrust can occasion no real surprise.
We already know that his refusal of free hospitality
constitutes ipso facto a repudiation of the intimacy
that had previously obtained between the two. Since
this, in turn, presupposes substantial abuse of friendship in the past, it is only natural that we should now
find our poet wary of fresh injury. When all is said,
therefore, the spirit of haggling reproach which marks
this ode must be referred to the uses of affection, in
which, as Horace represents them, Vergil has been
remiss.

We must now be prepared to see that the affection
in question is, in fact, erotic. The possibility, it
should be noted, is not new to classical scholarship.
Nisbet and Hubbard have dealt with it at least so far as
to dismiss it out of hand. Specifically, they find the
traditional erotic nature of the propempticon "impossible" where Sic te diva, our key ode, is concerned; and
they detect only a "note of sober friendship" in the
phrase animae dimidium meae, despite the fact that it is
a precise translation of homosexual endearment that
traces back through Meleager to Callimachus.[15] If such
reasoning reflects scholarly detachment, then what is

bias? The fact is that these are only two of several
formidable considerations favoring an erotic interpretation of 1:3. It is time that we confront them, each
and all, without regard for irrelevant proprieties.

First, one further architectural consideration.
The Europa ode, the only other propempticon in the
collection, occurs fourth from the end of Book III.
Already a reasonably precise balance with Sic te diva
emerges, and, if, after the manner of the propempticon,
the latter turns out to be erotic as well, the equi-
poise becomes nigh perfect. In due course we shall
find that the correspondence runs even deeper than this.

Now let us turn to Sic te diva itself. Its very
first evocation is of the powerful goddess of love,
diva potens Cypri. Next, Helen's name, appearing by no
contextual necessity, enters to enrich the ambience of
erotic suggestiveness. Then the symbolism comes into
play. The steady following wind (1. 4) indicates a
prospering passion, and the ship, which Venus herself
will share in guiding, readily suggests the phallus.
But the ship is at the same time so far personified as
to possess a kind of will of its own. As with Horace
in O Navis, therefore, it is feasibly taken to represent
Vergil himself, but Vergil sexually identified, while
the ode's occasion may be understood to reflect nothing
more or less than a juncture in the relationship between
the two poets when Vergil sets off on a conventional
erotic adventure.[16] Horace wishes him fair success,
but only on the condition that the "half of his heart"
return wholly to him once more.

All of this and more comes to light in the first
two stanzas:

> Sic te diva potens Cypri
>   Sic fratres Helenae, lucida sidera,
> ventorumque regat pater
>   obstrictis aliis praeter Iapyga,
>
> navis quae tibi creditum
>   debes Vergilium; finibus Atticis
> reddas incolumem, precor,
>   et serves animae dimidium meae.

The Latin has proved stubborn. In its essentials, the standard translation runs, "On this condition may the gods favor you . . . O ship that owe me Vergil, deliver him up to Attic shores . . . ". Syndikus demurs, arguing with merit that the re- of reddas is in that case obtrusive. He accordingly translates, " . . . O ship that owe Vergil to Attic shores, return him to me . . . ".[17] This has the virtue of emphasizing the restoration of the traveler to the poet, which is a standing topos of the propempticon, but is itself somewhat awkward. I favor construing finibus Atticis as ablative, and I translate:

> On this condition may the potent
> Cyprian goddess and those bright stars,
> Helen's brothers, and the father of the
> winds, confining all except Iapyx, guide
> you, O ship, that owe me Vergil, entrusted
> to your care: restore him to me safely
> from Attic shores and preserve the half
> of my heart.

The greatest difficulty with the standard translation is that it offers an insipid quid pro quo: on this condition do I wish you a fair voyage--that you enjoy a fair voyage.[18] By contrast, insistence on restora-

tion makes for an eminently sensible exchange of benefits. But it also contains a challenging implication.
We gather that, unless Vergil is safely restored, Horace could not care less what troubles beset the ship.
This would constitute a graceless excess were we dealing with an actual voyage. Not only would Vergil be
lost, but he must suffer certain tribulation besides.
But if, as I suggest, the issue which Horace confronts
is actually the prospect of erotic abandonment, and if
the ship is ultimately the phallus, such callousness
falls readily into place. Why wish a lover's act of
betrayal godspeed?[19]

At the same time, the interjected <u>precor</u> (<u>1</u>. 7)
exposes Horace's acute vulnerability. Sped straight
from the heart, woefully incongruous with his tone of
tough-minded negotiation, it betrays a desperate pre-
possession: Vergil's return is all that really matters.

Hereupon by degrees the poem appears to swerve
completely out of orbit. Starting with an ambivalent
condemnation of the first sailor, the poet proceeds to
deplore the entire human impulse toward enterprise,
singling out along the way some of the world's most
brilliant heroes for special reprehension, and ends by
blasting the whole as <u>scelus</u>. Startled and dismayed,
scholars have tended to score the performance vigorous-
ly, while apologists have, if anything, aggravated the
perplexity.[20] Such are the wages of refusing the ode's
amatory design.

The poem indeed veers off into irrationality, but
for purposes that are really quite transparent. Underlying Horace's obvious concerns--for Vergil's safety,
for his return and the preservation of his love--is a

fundamental anxiety over the fact of separation itself.
This is all the more intense in that (lest it be
molestum) it must be disguised. What is more natural
than for such feelings to find expression in deflected
form? This is the key to our poem. Horace can summon
up qualified blessings for Vergil's adventure, but at
heart he disapproves of it mightily. Gradually, inevitably, his resentment surfaces and burgeons into a
tirade aimed ostensibly at mankind's damnable restless-
ness, but actually against Vergil's, his beloved's, who,
unable to remain content at his side, now leaves him
wretchedly behind. It is all a childish transport, no
doubt; but so is Eros a child.

We run a bit ahead of ourselves, however. We have
seen that at the beginning of the ode Horace erects a
facade of tough-mindedness which is immediately comprised
by an interjection of entreaty. Just so does emotion
win out over the artifice of self-control in the long
second section of the poem. In his description of the
first sailor (9-20), Horace exclaims over the extraordinary courage of the man who first "entrusted his
fragile raft to the savage sea" and harbored no fear of
warring winds or "floating monsters." This, the most
fully realized symbolic passage in the ode, is, I think,
best understood as an attempt at sophisticated jocula-
rity. Symbolically the passage describes the man who
first essayed the sexual nature of woman. As such, it
could be strictly monitory, of course, but the passage
seems weighted with too much exaggeration both on the
literal and symbolic levels for such a function. Was
the first sailor truly so bold? Would his daring
plausibly have argued that he had prevailed over the

fear of death (17ff.). Ought he indeed to have wept at
the sight of "floating prodigies" (1. 18)? Much less
the first lover. By such persiflage, then, he momentarily regains a semblance of poise, only to lose it
once and for all to the surge of discontent already
noted.

We have so far been preoccupied with the complement
which 4:12 provides to Sic te diva. What of the ode's
elaboration in the primary edition? Here Horace's touch
is more than usually subtle, but still certain. There
is no Vergil ode at the close of III to offset the
work's beginning, but there is a propempticon, Impios
parrae (3:27) some of whose affinities to Sic te diva
we have already noticed. Two further points of correspondence are particularly revealing. First, the ode
opens with a burst of curses for the impios who would go
on journeys--all but the precise note on which Sic te
diva ended. Now, we will recall, Vergil was expressly
termed pius at 1:24, 11. Might Horace not intend an
ironic interplay between that epithet and the emphatic
Impios here? Bearing in mind that Impios parrae is the
only propempticon among the Odes besides Sic te diva,
let us trace the idea of piety through these three
pieces. As a plea, essentially, for fidelity, Sic te
diva begs pietas from Vergil, or, on the sterner side,
admonishes him of his pious obligations. Next (1:24),
Vergil is freely termed pius, and that in an ode which
deeply stresses the bond of friendship. So far, so
good.[21] But then, while resuming not only the propempticon form, but the very theme of scelus through which
he had protested against his abandonment in 1:3, Horace
aims a withering condemnation against the impious

traveler. Just as surely as the one context resumes the
other, it implicates Vergil--the only traveler remotely
in question--as well. It would seem, then, that Horace's worst fears have already been realized; and, moreover, between the pius of 1:24 and the impios here, we
have a first hint of that drastic change in Horace's
personal esteem for Vergil which comes clear in 4:12.

The second detail firms these up to the letter.
At 18ff. Horace warns Galatea:

> Ego quid sit ater
>   Hadriae novi sinus et quid albus
>   peccet Iapyx.

> I know what the black gulf of
> the Adriatic is like and I know the
> treachery of Iapyx.

He otherwise mentions Iapyx only in 1:3, where, however, he did not question its benignity. Is it sensible
to suppose that his altered opinion derives from any
other experience than its behavior on that occasion?
In a word, it proved peccator. Thus once more a change
from fair to foul and once more the theme of scelus;
only this time it is the symbolism which inculpates
Vergil. Wind translates symbolically into emotion, and
a happy wind (the Iapyx of 1:3) which, encountering no
opposition, speeds the lover surely to his goal translates into the felicitous force of his own erotic
inspiration. This ventus albus Horace had (in the
poetry's own "commercial" terms) traded away on trust
upon Vergil's symbolic passage to Greece, but, turning
traitor, it blew more potently than had been bargained

129

for. Without rejecting the possibility that Vergil himself might have been among its casualties, we cannot
mistake that Horace feels himself its chief dupe and
victim. He would seem to range himself, in fact, with
Pyrrha's hapless lover, who was similarly _credulus_
where his beloved's emotions were concerned and, above
all, _nescius aurae fallacis_. Thus, even on the evidence
of the first edition we must utterly doubt whether Horace ever received back _incolumem_ the "half of his heart."

It remains to survey the full corroborative testimony of _Iam veris comites_. That ode opens on the motif
of navigation, which, emitting its usual sexual-symbolic
overtones, strikes up an immediate rapport with 1:3.
Viewed as an easterly wind the _animae Thraciae_ (_l_. 2)
add a further element of harmony, for, just as Iapyx
ideally suits sailings to Greece, so do these breezes
foster the journey back. Hence, a notion of Vergil's
own return rises to mind. Even if, bowing to the
knotty ambivalence of the phrase, we despair of fixing
the wind's direction,[22] a ghost of the same idea yet
inheres. For, starting with references to Thrace,
Athens and Arcadia, the whole poem proceeds, in antithesis to _Sic te diva_, from the Greek world back to
Horace's own doorstep.

A more specific response to 1:3 comes with the
second stanza, where the ode's initial symbolic suggestions of erotic propitiousness (moderated seas, thawed
fields, gentled streams) suffer catastrophic reversal.
Athens, Vergil's symbolic destination in _Sic te diva_,
now figures as the setting of one of the ancient world's
most pathetic love tales. The general implications for
Vergil's erotic enterprises are plain enough, while the

specific emphases on Procne's regret and disgrace may
well be meant to mirror the effects of Vergil's own
implication in scelus. In any case, it is not lost
upon us that the leitmotif of the Tereus-Procne affair
is betrayal.

The Arcadian scene that ensues restores the calm
and, more fragilely, the erotic promise of the opening.
Its bright tableau of poets singing as one serves, first
of all, to recollect the unity of hearts between our own
two bards cited in Sic te diva. More propitiously
still, we would seem to have in the theme of concerted
music that enchants the woodland (and therefore phallic)
god the seeds of the kind of blended song that led
Horace and Lyde inevitably to Venus in Festo quid potius.

But it is not to be. The single heart has become
irrevocably two. Horace demands an earnest from his
"merchant" friend and, for his own part, offers only an
ironic affection in return. This is to say that, whatever his intimations, Horace does not invite intimacy
under any circumstances. The intimations are bright
enough (17ff.):

> Nardi parvus onyx eliciet cadum . . .
> spes donare novas largus amaraque
>   curarum eluere efficax.

> A small flask of nard will lure
> forth the cask . . . [which] is generous
> to bestow new hopes and able to wash
> away bitter cares.

Neither the onyx nor the cadum, both symbolically feminine, resists an homoerotic interpretation, while the

contrast of <u>largus</u> with <u>parvus</u> implies that Horace is
willing to contribute more than a <u>dimidium</u> toward a
renewal of old sympathies.

If this sounds more like conciliation than retribution for <u>scelus</u>, however, the impression soon fades.
We have postulated that Vergil's contribution of nard
is to serve as a proof of genuine commitment on his
side. But it becomes clear that Horace expects nothing
so grand from his wayward friend. After insisting anew
on a contribution and beckoning his adversary on, our
poet ends:

> . . . misce stultiam consiliis brevem;
> dulce est desipere in loco.

> . . . mix a brief folly into your
> plans; it is pleasant to play the fool
> when the time is right.

The <u>Odes</u> offers no specimen of irony more penetrating
than this. Horace asks of his friend only that degree
of intimacy which he has proved himself generous in
giving: a passing encounter. More pointedly, the word
<u>consiliis</u> can only imply the "merchant's" wonted de-
signs, inspired by his <u>studium lucri</u>, of exploitation.
This, it is plain, is not merely to charge <u>scelus</u>, but
to pronounce it incorrigible. And the burden of
<u>stultitiam</u>, compounded by its equivalent, <u>desipere</u>,
drives the barb even further home. At the close of <u>Sic
te diva</u>, Horace equated <u>stultitia</u>, against the background of Vergil's waywardness, with <u>scelus</u>:

> caelum ipsum petimus stultitia, neque
> per nostrum patimur scelus
> iracunda Iovem ponere fulmina.

> The sky itself we strive for in
> our folly, nor, through our corruption,
> do we permit Jupiter to lay aside his
> furious thunderbolt.

It follows that his stultitia there amounts to his
consilia here and that neither is distinguishable from
the present stultitia. What, then, does it mean for
Vergil to interrupt his inveterate foolishness with "a
brief folly", or to desipere in loco? A reduction in
scale, perhaps, but that merely crowns the mockery.
In sum, compromised utterly by his faithlessness, Vergil's loves have lost all meaning, and it is strictly
to expose their emptiness that Horace extends an inane
intimacy.

Thus for the second time in the final book the
variegated promise of emerging spring founders in resignation. In Diffugere nives it was the shadow of mortality that discouraged enthusiasm. Here it is the
experience of the heart's inconstancy. We may now see
that 4:12 adds a further dimension to the Torquatus
ode's sense of cosmic isolation. Not only does the all-
devouring cycle of nature destine us to isolation, but
the fragility of human affections dooms love's allevia-
ting promise to defeat as well. And the two odes meld
yet further into one. Horace's advice in Diffugere
nives was gratification for the amico animo. There we
inferred the meaning that, among the affections, self-
love alone is substantial. The phrase equally suggests

that one's self is one's only meaningful friend--that there can be no such thing as a "half of one's heart."

This understood, we can better surmise why, after forebearing at the close of III, Horace implicated Vergil by name in such a compromising context after his death. It was not to save his brother poet embarrassment while he lived. Rather, by 23 B.C. Horace had not yet arrived at the conviction of love's insubstantiality that beset him later on. Once he did, his relationship with Vergil, his most intimate love, became the obviously right vehicle of its expression.

While I regret that certain aspects of our argument may offend some admirers of Vergil, I feel that Horace himself made adequate reparation with the last words of the Odes. A poet's work, after all, is his essential reputation, and Vergil's accomplishments were never more meaningfully admired than in those parting accents.

Meanwhile, the argument offers nothing that is categorically new. The imputation of homosexuality, we must remember, is as old as Servius, who identified the Corydon and Alexis of the second Eclogue as, respectively, Vergil himself and a boy named Alexander whom the poet had accepted as a gift from Pollio. And, as for moral laxity in general, a newly discovered Vita Vergiliana of the ninth century ranges unimaginably further than anything suggested herein:

> De vita autem poetae pauca sunt dicenda
> quia nec talis fuit ut imitari debeat
> nec ut in aeterna memoria reponi debeat.[23]

As for the poet's life, little
ought to be said, since it was not such
as deserves to be imitated or commemorated
for all time.

The only value of such innuendo is to remind us that we
lack the hard evidence to refute it.

CHAPTER FIVE
THE PATRIOTIC ODES

Judging from the frequency with which he shies
away from martial themes, one must account Horace averse
on very principle to the heroic strain in lyric poetry.
Similarly, his declared preference for light, witty and,
indeed, slight lyrics argues against any deep-rooted
interest in political, social or ethical subjects.
Still, a goodly proportion of his lyrical creations
occupy themselves with just this range of themes. How
can we explain the paradox? The cynical response is
that he was constrained to produce patriotic poems,
even to the point of abetting official propaganda. Obviously, we cannot rule out the pressures of patronage
altogether. Without them, Horace would likely have pro-
duced less impressive an array of such odes. But there
is equally little doubt that he found the task of composing them congenial enough.

First, the Epicurean in him would have found
Augustus' provision of peace and security consummately
worthy of celebration. Second, it is plain that he took
deep pride in the Roman achievement from Romulus onward
and, at the same time, regarded with genuine revulsion
the degeneracy that he detected in his own time across
the whole spectrum of ancestral virtues. Also, he was

evidently susceptible by nature to the glory that such
poetry held out for its distinguished practitioners.
The fourth book (where the proportion of patriotic
themes is, not surprisingly, densest) finds him frankly
enchanted with the distinction, ratified by his selection to compose the Carmen Saeculare, of having become
Rome's poet laureate. On top of all this, he here and
there lets fall indications that, all along, he considered this strain of lyric of a higher order than those
composed, as he claimed he was strictly suited to compose, Dionaeo sub antro--"in Venus' cave."

But a consideration equal in importance to any of
these is that he could adapt his muse to patriotic
poetry without radical change of manner or method. Not
only did he find ample place in this "other" verse for
the full palette of his lighter lyrics, but, more
particularly, he was able to continue composing--less
often, perhaps, but not less tellingly--Dionaeo sub
antro. Thus it is that even here symbolic expressionism
continues to keep company with the most potent resources
of his art.

Moreover, the symbolism's conceptual frame of
reference remains substantially intact. If a philosophy
of behavior runs through the erotic odes, it is that, as
a matter of common sense, the sexual impulse must be
honored, but subject to the control of reason. The
political analogue to the fund of emotional energy comprised on the personal level by sexuality is the innate
martial frenzy that, on its positive side, made Rome
great, but, turned inward in the recent civil wars, all
but brought her down. We speak here, of course, of
virtus in its rawest manifestation as brute physical

137

prowess. For Horace, this stupendous _vis_ requires
temperance, the control of _consilium_, if it is to become instructed virtue and so eventuate in justice and
peace. It needs, as it turns out, an Augustus, who,
as we shall see, operates in his most sublime configura-
tion in the _Odes_ as the preserving _nous_ of the Roman
state--though at whose higher guidance he does so comes
as an exalting Horatian surprise. Thus, just as the
ordinary individual preserves himself from his own
passions by prudent self-control, so is the community
kept harmoniously intact by wise governance at its head.
For us the crucial point is that, even on the political
level, the passionate aspect, both in its creative and
destructive potential, is consistently expressed in
sexual terms and these largely symbolic.

This being a different order of poetry, however, the
symbolism is put to a more limited kind of work. In the
patriotic odes the symbolism always supports the leading
theme, often subtly, of course, and sometimes with the
effect of epiphany, but we see little of the delight in
mystification, much less in metamorphism, that plays
through the erotic odes. Also, the range of symbolic
images is somewhat less varied than in those odes.
These are mere adjustments of technique, however, and
only one radical difference subsists. The erotic odes
offer, and mean to offer, no great case for virile
potency. Where strength is concerned, it is the female,
epitomized in the magnificent Pyrrha, but also well rendered in a Barine, a Lydia and others, who excels. But
rarely, of course, do her powers win her positive dignity. This entire arrangement is greatly altered in
the patriotic odes. Though woman largely remains an

object of distrust, she also attains to superlative dignity. Equally so the phallus; and far more so on
grounds of frequency of representation. Indeed, it may
be said that the most pervasive sexual-symbolic motif in
these odes centers on the notion of phallic prowess.
That which is crude and debasing in such a stimulus is
taken fully into account. But Horace also finds therein much that is sublime, the more so as he grew older,
so that, of all the symbolic motifs at work in the
patriotic odes of the first three books, scarcely anything else survives in the like pieces of Book IV.

One reason for its perseverance is already distinct enough. If Horace's rallying cry in the patriotic
odes is for the realization of virtus, and if, at its
etymological roots, virtus signifies virile prowess,
where would our poet have assigned its symbolic expression if not to adumbrations of the phallus?

At the expense of his poet friend Valgius, Horace
in Non semper imbres (2:9) leads us through the very
turn from erotic to patriotic poetry that now confronts
us. Valgius has been writing elegy after elegy lament-
ing the loss of his pederastic favorite, Mystes. Horace
admonishes him by paradigms drawn first from nature and
then from instances of human bereavement that no grief
rightly lasts forever.

Rains do not perpetually plague the meadows, he
begins, nor winds the seas; neither is ice perpetual in
Armenia, nor (6f.):

> . . . Aquilonibus
> querceta Gargani laborant
> et foliis viduantur orni.

139

> . . . are the oak groves of Garganus
> always toiling under the North winds and
> the ashes stripped of their leaves.

Horace's point is not merely that the weather changes
with the seasons. The symbolic burden of the tree
images, bolstered by the feminine imagery of water and
field earlier on, argue that love's weather also changes.
But Valgius is immune to any such lessons (9ff.):

> . . . tu semper urges flebilibus modis
> Mysten ademptum, nec tibi Vespero
> surgente decedunt amores nec
> rapidum fugiente solem.

> . . . You continually ply your lost
> Mystes with mournful measures, and your
> loves subside neither when Vesper rises
> nor when he flees the swift-faring sun.

Hence, Valgius perseveres in a grief that finds no
parallel in nature, and we may agree with Commager that
Horace thereby scores a point against the elegiac manner
in general.[1] But the real strength of the passage lies
in its psychological texture, which is fully accessible
only in the symbolism. The mention of Vesper alerts us
to Horace's drift. This is the love star--whose risings
and settings likewise have no influence with Valgius.
Then, both the word _urges_ in its sexual shading and the
play on night-long _amores_ impart the notion of veritable
physical possession. The unnaturalness of Valgius'
pertinacity is thus vastly heightened by the hint that
it actually enacts an unconscious prolongation of his
intimacy with Mystes.

If astringent, the sentiment is not cruel. Valgius'
state calls for strong remedies. After the further admonition that neither Antilochus nor Troilus was mourned
forever, Horace prescribes a specific cure (17ff.):

> Desine mollium
> tandem querellarum et potius nova
>   cantemus Augusti tropaea Caesaris et
>   rigidum Niphaten,
>
> Medumque flumen gentibus additum
> victis minores volvere vertices,
>   intraque praescriptum Gelonos
>   exiguis equitare campis.

>   Leave off your soft laments at last
> and, rather, let us sing the new trophies
> of Caesar, stiff Niphates and the Persian
> river that, added to the nations subdued,
> now churns up lesser waves, and the
> Geloni, who ride within stricter bounds,
> their territories shrunken.

The key terms for us are mollium and rigidum, though they
scarcely seem to correlate on the primary level. Valgius'
laments are "soft" because they are unmanly in every
nuance of the term. Niphates is "stiff" because--as best
the commentators can make out--that mountain is ever
snow-capped. The two epithets correlate sexually, however, and with a wonderful relevancy: flaccid effeminacy on the one hand and majestic manliness on the other.
Figuratively as well as literally, then, Horace prescribes
a more manly occupation of Valgius' muse. But the manliness also attaches to Augustus and his essential virtus.
     To round things off, Horace resumes the imagery of
waters and earth at the beginning, but here these are

qualified as humbled and restricted. Symbolically, this
implies the conquest of woman, the ultimate proof of
phallic prowess.

On the heels of <u>Non</u> <u>semper</u> <u>imbres</u> arrives a second
ode premised on the phenomenon of change, the graceful
and famous ode to Licinius. Its sexual-symbolic into-
nations are so pervasive that one might conclude it to
be addressed as intimately to Licinius' love life as was
the previous ode to Valgius'. Doubtless, however, its
prime target is Licinius' political volatility. But it
is also a sexual scherzo. To illustrate the hoary theme
of the wisdom of moderation by a string of sexually-
tinted metaphors, and to carry it all off without seeming to miss a beat of moral solemnity, is pretty amusement. If the reader misses the fun, well and good. He
has gotten the sermon he has come for. If not, he has
been treated to an interlude of high Horatian music.
Our particular interest, however, lies in the turnabout
from the previous ode where phallic prowess is concerned:

> Rectius vives, Licini, neque altum
> semper urgendo neque, dum procellas
> cautus horrescis, nimium premendo
>   litus iniquum.
>
> Auream quisquis mediocritatem
> diligit, tutus caret obsoleti
> sordibus tecti, caret invidenda
>   sobrius aula.
>
> Saepius ventis agitatur ingens
> pinus et celsae graviore casu
> decidunt turres feriuntque summos
>   fulgura montis.
>
> Sperat infestis, metuit secundis
> alteram sortem bene praeparatum

pectus. Informis hiemes reducit
    Iuppiter, idem

summovet. Non, si male nunc, et olim
sic erit: quondam cithara tacentem
suscitat Musam neque semper arcum
    tendit Apollo.

Rebus angustis animosus atque
fortis appare; sapienter idem
contrahes vento nimium secundo
    turgida vela.

    You will live more uprightly,
Licinius, by neither constantly plying
the deep, nor, while carefully shunning
the stormblasts, hugging the rugged shore
too closely. Whoever loves the golden
mean prudently avoids the squalor of a
dilapidated house and wisely, too, shuns
the envied hall. Generally, it is the
huge pine that is rocked by the winds and
the lofty tower that collapses with the
heaviest crash, and lightning smites the
mountain tops. The well-prepared heart
hopes for a change of fortune when things
are adverse and fears it when they prosper.
Jupiter brings back the ugly winter; he
also removes it. If things go badly now,
it will not be so anon. Apollo sometimes
awakens the slumbering muse with his lyre
and does not always stretch his bow. Show
yourself brave and doughty in straitened
circumstances; but you will also be wise
to trim your swollen sails when the wind
blows too favorably.

Despite the compelling metronomic effect, the poem's
rhetorical rhythm is not strictly antithetic. The third
stanza, devoted wholly to the idea that to be outsized
is to be vulnerable, makes prosperity--on the symbolic

side, phallic prosperity--the extreme among life's
changes most to beware. In preponderant effect, then,
the ode's symbolic advice is most familiar: fear emasculation. This abrupt retreat from the evocations of
rigidum Niphaten a moment ago marks a distinction which
Horace regularly keeps in his patriotic odes. Grandeur
and aggressive might, resplendent virtues where the
state is concerned and the cause of its prosperity, are
at best precarious attributes of the private individual
and, at worst, symptoms of corruption. He offers two
moral diatribes in illustration.

It is private grandeur which bears the brunt of
Horace's scorn in Iam pauca aratro (2:15). The fact
that the ode's sentiments harmonize perfectly with the
emperor's official aversion to private luxury makes it
without question a political, even a propagandistic piece.
But the warmth of the poet's repugnance indicates that
he speaks from personal conviction as well:

> Iam pauca aratro iugura regiae
> moles relinquent, undique latius
>   extenta visentur Lucrino
>   stagna lacu, platanusque caelebs
>
> evincet ulmos; tum violaria et
> myrtus et omnis copia narium
>   spargent olivetis odorem
>   fertilibus domino priori;
>
> tum spissa ramis laurea fervidos
> excludet ictus. Non ita Romuli
>   praescriptum et intonsi Catonis
>   auspiciis veterumque norma.
>
> Privatus illis census erat brevis.
> commune magnum: nulla decempedis

metata privatis opacam
porticus excipiebat Arcton,

nec fortuitum spernere caespitem
leges sinebant, oppida publico
sumptu iubentes et deorum
templa novo decorare saxo.

Soon high-piled palaces fit for a
king will leave few acres for the plow
and fishpools spreading wider than the
Lucrine lake will appear everywhere and
the bachelor plane will crowd out the
elms; then violets and myrtles and the
whole company of sweet perfumes will
spread their aroma in olive groves that
yielded fruit for their former master;
then dense-branched laurel will shut out
the warm sunrays. Not thus was it prescribed under the rule of Romulus and
unshorn Cato and by the ancestral standard. Their income was small, the
commonwealth enormous. No portico
measured out for private occupants by
ten-foot poles lay open to the shady
north, nor did the laws permit them to
scorn the ubiquitous turf in building
their dwellings, while ordering them to
embellish their towns at public cost and
their temples of the gods with new-cut
stone.

The pervasive literal indictment of idle extravagance attains sharper point by an extended symbolic play
on sexual sterility. That notion comes through clearly
both on the literal and figurative levels in the detail
of the plane shouldering out the elm: to the elm is
wed the vine; the plane exists for pleasure alone.
Similarly, the high-piled palaces, which in this ode,
as we shall see, are phallic, are displacing the phallic

145

and useful plow. On the female side, the artificial and
absurdly wide-spread fishpools strike the same symbolic
chord of inutile extravagance. But the main symbolic
extravaganza is displayed in the enormous, shade-
nestled porticoes. By virtue of the boldly quantitative
ascription <u>decempedis</u> we see the huge columns ascend,
<u>as</u> <u>if</u> the columns of magnificent public temples, into
sheer inanity. Here stands the precious, sterile
phallus, and herein are exposed the idle rich in all
their ignobility.

The venom is even deadlier in <u>Non ebur neque</u>
<u>aureum</u> (2:18). My ceilings are not golden or ivoried,
the poet proclaims, nor have I inherited Attalus'
palace; but I have my talent, reputation and unique
Sabine farm, and I ask for nothing more. He then turns
to a nameless, boundlessly rich addressee who asks, as
it turns out, for the impossible (15ff.):

> Truditur dies die
> > novaeque pergunt interire lunae.
>
> Tu secanda marmora
> > locas sub ipsum funus et sepulcri
> immemor struis domos
> > marisque Bais obstrepentis urges
>
> summovere litora,
> > parum locuples continente ripa.
> Quid quod usque proximos
> > revellis agri terminos et ultra
>
> limites clientium
> > salis avarus? Pellitur paternos
> in sinu ferens deos
> > et uxor et vir sordidosque natos.
>
> Nulla certior tamen
> > rapacis Orci fine destinata

aula divitem manet
        erum. Quid ultra tendis?

        Day is thrust aside by day, and new
moons hasten to perish. You let contracts
for cutting marble on the very brink of
death and, mindless of the grave, you
strain to push out the shore of the sea
resounding against Baiae, insufficiently
rich so long as the coast hems you in.
What of the fact that, one by one, you
tear up the margin-stones of your farm,
and, in your greed, overleap the bound-
aries of your clients? Both wife and
husband are driven off, bearing in their
arms their ancestral gods and their ragged
children. Yet no surer hall awaits the
rich lord than the destined bound of
rapacious Orcus. Why do you strive to go
beyond?

Thus, the poem turns on the idea of observing limit.
Horace does; his aged addressee does not. He therefore
encroaches upon the limits of land, sea and, by the
same violent, but futile impulse, time. For if we ask
why the frenzied old man is building a pleasure palace
within the very shadow of death, we must agree with
Commager that it is in the vain hope of escaping that
shadow.[2]

    The frenzy itself attains its most vivid moment on
the symbolic level. Sea and land being both symbolically
feminine, forcible encroachment thereon intimates sexual
aggression. Between the two, the figure is more fully
developed in the imagery of trespass upon the sea.
Urges and summovere (we recall urget grato sub antro
from the Pyrrha ode) contribute their unmistakable
parts; and we may perhaps detect in maris obstrepantis

147

a feminine cry of protest against the violent act of
intrusion. In any case, with a determined thrust of
his absurd promontory the senseless old party will take
by assault--ultimately from time--that which none may
touch. We shall presently hear of the abject principle
underlying such behavior in a much statelier ode.

Has such asperity been taken sufficiently into
account in assessing Horace's performance in the patriotic odes? I suggest that anyone scanning these
offerings in the first three books for signs of definitive confidence in Rome's future is likely to meet with
disappointment. Not only is Horace's tone frequently
as critical as in the pair of odes just noted, but his
scorn extends more liberally to excesses of public
behavior. It may be argued that this is singularly
unsurprising, seeing that one of the emperor's dearest
objectives was the state's moral reform. And does not
Horace promote Augustus as precisely the man-greater-
than-man capable of executing such a reformation? Perhaps he does; but neither must we search very hard for
signs of despair. If then, Horace does indeed leave
doubts concerning Rome's future as of 23 B.C., we may
have a fresh perspective on the question of the independence and objectivity of his political judgment. At
all events, we had best start with the survey just
proposed.

Horace addresses the question of Rome's future at
the first opportunity possible (_Iam_ _satis_ _terris_, 1:2).
After deploring the civil wars, he calls for a divine
expiator and settles upon Augustus, who thereby acquires his first delicate tints of divinity, as the
champion both suited to accomplish that task and to

chastize Rome's enemies as well. So far so good,
though the reader is left with a heavy impression of
internecine crime.

Despite this robust start, the first book is not
much given to patriotic issues. Only three further
odes figure seriously in this category. Two are major,
ringing eulogies of Augustus.[3] In Quem virum aut heroa
(1:12), the emperor, much as his persona is blended
into that of Mercury in Iam satis terris, is compared
to Jupiter himself, only more daringly.[4] The father of
the gods is first (l. 18) pronounced so eminent that no
other divinity can be considered "similar or second" to
him. Then (51f.), crowning a roll-call of select Roman
heroes, Augustus is graced with a position of rule
second to Jupiter, his destined guardian.[5] Breathtaking
eulogy, this. Also, the ode closes with the crucial
notice that Augustus will be conqueror in his own right
and, as the god's beneficiary, reformer, the last office
making a first reference to the severe social ills that
beset the state.

O diva gratum (1:35) breaks into the series of
eulogies to exclaim plangently upon the political and
social vices that Horace has so far sketched (33ff.).
The scars of civil strife are cause for shame, cries
the poet, and he goes on to lament that the iniquitous
age, stopping at no sacrilege, has put fear of the gods
behind it. We may take note that he singles out the
Roman youth (iuventus, l. 36) for particular censure in
this regard.

Finally, the Cleopatra ode (1:37) gives us Augustus
the conqueror as nowhere else in the Odes. Formally,
meanwhile, it closes the circle with 1:2 and 1:12 on

several thematic levels. It depicts the victory at
Actium, which brought an end to civil strife, as at the
same time a conquest over degeneracy and excess. We
thus may again attribute to Augustus the twin function
of conquest and reform. Concurrently, it represents
Augustus as foiling a threat to the capital quite as
Jupiter had himself in Iam satis terris (1. 18). All
the more are we encouraged to regard the emperor as a
"second Jupiter."

Were it not for the impassioned outburst in O diva
gratum, then, we might say that the first book presents
a strong and orderly case for political optimism. But,
in fact, it propounds a conundrum. What deliverance is
there even in the appearance of a "second Jupiter" if
the Roman citizenry has lost every vestige of respect
for the gods? More to our present issue, what hope is
there for the future if the Roman youth has proved itself the most godless of all? Clearly, the solution of
the social predicament requires a degree of inspired
leadership that, for all the glorification of Augustus,
has not yet been attested.

The second book, if anything, takes a small step
backward. The very first ode raises again the issue of
the civil wars, deploring the fact that every corner of
the world testifies to those impia proelia (29ff.).
The book's main patriotic issue, however, concerns not
political but social problems. In Iam pauca aratro and
Non ebur neque aureum we have already witnessed two of
its indictments of the distortions that wealth breeds.
Though milder in tone, Nullus argento (2:2) also belongs
to that list. Only the Valgius ode with its celebration
of the emperor's victories stands on the positive side

of the ledger. Thus, once more Augustus the conqueror.
He receives no notice as a reformer, however, much less
a divinely inspired reformer.

Then come the Roman Odes, the first six poems, all
in the identical, weighty meter, of Book III, in which
both Horace's hopes and fears for the future reach their
ripest expression. The divine Augustus again emerges as
champion of a new order, and, what is more, the structure of the sextet lends his appearances--brief enough
in themselves--the utmost authority. Yet, side by side
with these heartening evocations exists evidence, likewise emphasized by structure, of despair.

Commager feels that the third Roman Ode addresses
the future more squarely than any political poem of the
first three books, and he finds little standing in the
way of a coming millenium: "All that was now needed
was for Augustus to show his constantia and iustitia in
ruling both his people and himself. . . . ".[6] But if,
as Commager himself brilliantly argues, Juno's injunction
against the resuscitation of Troy (37ff.; 57ff.) signifies a demand that Augustan Rome renounce "all the evil
elements of the past," then the question of Horace's own
optimism is open to grave doubt. And does not Delicta
maiorum (3:6) find him still haunted by ancestral crimes?
Closer to home, the third ode itself places a heavy
qualification on future prosperity. Juno's vision of
Rome's eventual greatness--and the context makes it
clear that the future in question is that of Augustan
Rome--is predicated on a moral piety that will restrain
the Roman citizenry from seeking wealth and, generally,
from plundering that which is sacred (49ff.). Yet, if
the first three books pass any judgment on Roman society,

151

it is that it will never give up its corrupting thirst
for gold. Otherwise, Commager is more tentative than
he needs to be. Seeing that Augustus' constantia and
iustitia will make him divine (10f.), he will surely
practice those virtues in governing his people and himself; and, since these same virtues will enable him to
withstand the resistance of a corrupt citizenry (l. 2),
we deduce the implication that he will indeed one day
carry through the social reformation that will ratify
Juno's vision. But the optimism lasts only so long as
the ode lasts. This side of the fourth book, it is in
the very nature of the patriotic odes that every swell
of confidence be countervailed by a surge of misgiving--
all, as we shall see, save one, and even then the
counsels of hopelessness are never quite stilled.

    Both the negative and positive accents of the
Roman Odes yield most readily to an architectonic over-
view. The sextet opens thus:

        Odi profanum vulgus et arceo;
        favete linguis: carmina non prius
           audita Musarum sacerdos
                virginibus puerisque canto.

        I despise the uninitiate throng
        and hold it at a distance; keep a
        reverent tongue: priest of the muses,
        I sing for girls and boys songs never
        heard before.

If there is a trace of amusement in our poet's appearance in priestly garb, it soon fades. The metaphor is
quite in earnest. Horace is certainly serious about the
originality of his lyrics; and if we want to know with

some precision who the "uninitiate throng" might be, we are led to the inescapable conclusion that they include all except the very young, the girls and boys who alone are invited to enter that suggestive temple of the muses which these six odes comprise. Why only the very young? Evidently because they alone are uncontaminated enough with the corruptions of the times to enter: and certainly because it is they who will inherit Rome. If there is to be a moral reformation for the state, then, Horace has deliberately taken it upon himself to sow its seeds in these odes. Not merely priest, he is educator as well, and none but the muses are his sacred source of wisdom. Without doubt, the poet nowhere else sets himself so bold and momentous a task.

After the introductory piece, which we will study more closely in a moment, the Roman Odes steadily ascend to the magnificent heights of Descende caelo (3:4) and then dismayingly back to earth. Meanwhile, they cleave to a nice axial-symmetry. The second ode summons Roman youth to the practice of virtus for his country: dulce et decorum est pro patria mori. The third, after predicting a like destiny for Augustus, has Juno consent to the deification of Romulus, thus saving Rome from divine wrath. The fourth, the center and hub of the six lyrics, locates a tranquil Augustus at the very fount of civilized inspiration.[7] But then the fifth, though it again stresses Augustus' divine destiny, bears down on the degeneracy of the modern Roman soldier. And in Delicta maiorum (3:6), Horace is sterner still. After linking certain military disasters to the citizenry's neglect of the gods, he condemns the defilement of the institutions of home, marriage and the family, whence,

he argues, all manner of public ills have flowed. So
much for the delicta maiorum, the crimes of previous
generations. He now turns a baleful eye upon the young
marrieds of his own time, charging them, but more so
the youthful bride, with rank connubial depravity.
Finally, the ode's unrelenting march through the generations carries even into the future. The sextet closes
thus:

> Aetas parentum peior avis tulit
>   nos nequiores mox daturos
>   progeniem vitiosiorem.

> Our parents' generation, worse
> than our grandparents', has born us,
> more worthless still, who will soon
> beget offspring more corrupt than
> ourselves.

Nothing in the Odes has been more undervalued than the
effect of this sentiment. If we take Horace at his
word, the very girls and boys whom he had chosen for his
exclusive pupils are by birth and contamination utterly
impervious to his teachings.

But this will never do, and, as we know, it is to
the center that we must look for climactic point in
Augustan poetry. Here the prospect is infinitely
brighter. Descende caelo is flanked and offset in the
third and fifth odes not only by the balancing references
to a deified Augustus just noticed, but also by other
conspicuous formal and substantive counterweights.
First, as Fraenkel observes, the set speeches that comprise the bulk both of 3:3 and 3:5 themselves provide a
formal frame for the fourth ode.[8] More pertinent, both

154

speeches are explicitly designated pieces of counsel
(3:3, 17f.; 3:5, 45f.), thereby pointing up the theme
of consilium, which, we shall presently see, is the
core issue of the pivotal fourth ode. We further note
that in the third ode the piece of counsel in question
is delivered to the gods in assembly, while in the fifth
the Roman senate is the audience. Thus, gods and men,
responding to consilia that in varying but profound ways
benefit and increase the Roman state set off Augustus,
the god-man, who, at the heart of Descende caelo (and,
thus, of the Roman Odes), imbibes the civilizing
consilium of the muses at the moment that he "seeks to
finish his labors." In context, these labors are unmistakably the works of peace. We can hardly imagine that
he will fail.

Still, the fifth and sixth odes raise billows of
doubt, which, moreover, are not nearly dispelled over
the balance of the book. Two odes of political significance remain. One (3:14) rather quietly reasserts the
positive impulses of the Roman Odes, while the other
(3:24) stages a last, monumental assault upon societal
vice. Since, therefore, Herculis ritu (3:14) offers
the last strains of political optimism in the primary
edition of the Odes, we had best analyze it fully here.

The ode marks Augustus' return from a successful
military venture in Spain. Horace calls upon the emperor's family, together with the mothers of the generation "just saved" by his victory to come forth and welcome him. He then turns to the youngsters themselves
(10ff.):

> Vos, o pueri et puellae
> iam virum expertae, male ominatis
> parcite verbis.
>
> Hic dies vere mihi festus atras
> eximet curas; ego nec tumultum
> nec mori per vim metuam tenente
> Caesare terras.
>
>
> You, o boys, and you girls who
> have now experienced a man, refrain
> from words of ill omen. This day,
> truly a festival for me, will lift
> my dark cares. I will neither fear
> tumult nor death by violence so long
> as Caesar rules the world.

This pointed inclusion of the young serves to recall
the opening of the Roman Odes, as does male ominatis
parcite verbis. More important, Horace's vow that he
will never fear violence while Caesar rules harks back
to Descende caelo, where it is indelibly established
that brute force is no match for the rationally informed
might that the emperor wields.

The balance of the ode, amusingly comparing minor
issues with great, recalls 3:4 as well. Horace sends
for Neaera to help ornament his private celebration of
the glad event, but instructs his servant-boy to back
off if the doorkeeper (a bit of sexual symbolism there)
proves difficult. He then closes (25ff.):

> Lenit albescens animos capillus
> litium et rixae cupidos protervae;
> non ego hoc ferrem calidus iuventa
> consule Planco.

> Whitening hair gentles spirits
> eager for quarrels and feisty brawling;
> I would not have endured this in my
> warm-blooded youth, when Plancus was
> consul.

The key words are <u>lenit</u> and <u>iuventa</u>. In 3:4 the Hecatoncheires, leading figures in the legendary rout of monsters and such that tried Jupiter's powers so sorely, are styled <u>iuventus</u> (<u>l</u>. 49); while the counsel which the muses impart and which always triumphs over such uncouth violence is emphatically <u>lene</u> (<u>l</u>. 41). The poet, then, in his grey-haired maturity has himself learned "<u>lene</u> <u>consilium</u>".[9] He has reformed. But what of the general Roman populace?

In <u>Intactis</u> <u>opulentior</u> (3.24), Horace attacks Roman society for its acquisitiveness, connubial depravity, rampant license, hatred of moral excellence, idle luxury, disrespect for law and custom and, most significantly, the corruption of its young. Towards the end of the ode, he calls for a revised manner of education--thereby recalling his purpose in the Roman Odes--founded in the procedures of the old school (51ff.):

> Eradenda cupidinis
> pravi sunt elementa et tenerae nimis
>
> mentes asperioribus
> formandae studiis. Nescit equo rudis
> haerere ingenuus puer
> venarique timet, ludere doctior
>
> seu Graeco iubeas trocho
> seu malis vetita legibus alea,
> cum periura patris fides
> consortem socium fallat et hospites,

> indignoque pecuniam
> heredi properet.

> The alphabet of perverted desire
> must be erased and the overly soft
> minds of the young must be shaped by
> sterner studies. Through lack of prac-
> tice the freeborn youth does not know
> how to stick to a horse and he fears to
> hunt, being more trained to sport with
> the Grecian hoop, if you bid him, or, if
> you prefer, with the dice forbidden by
> the laws, while his father's perjured
> word defrauds his business partner and
> makes haste to pass on pelf to a worth-
> less heir.

But, far from adding anything to the spirited call to
the traditional arts in 3:2, the entire approach in this
ode would seem to have lost touch with the erstwhile
lofty educational aim. At the very least, this last,
dispirited look at the Roman puer, the hope of the
state at the start of the Roman Odes, lends formidable
emphasis to the last, despairing look at him there
(3:6, 45ff.).

Nor does a study of the symbolic effects in the
patriotic odes dispel the gloom. Its results, as we
shall see, do indeed burnish the positive expectations
of Augustus' reign otherwise expressed, but the tension
between the emperor's remedial resources, inspired
though they are, and a society far gone down the road
to dissolution lingers on. Only with the fourth book is
the issue resolved in the emperor's absolute favor. But
that, together with its own attendant difficulties, must
wait its turn.

As the poet moves among great heroes of the Republi-

can past in <u>Quem virum aut heroa</u>, he inserts a sly
reference to Rome's future (1:12, 45f.):

> Crescit occulto velut arbor aevo
> fama Marcelli . . .

> The fame of Marcellus grows like
> a tree in the quiet passage of time . . .

In the immediate context, this refers to M. Claudius
Marcellus, a hero of the Second Punic War; but no con-
temporary reader would have missed an allusion to the
young Marcellus, who, except for his untimely death,
would have succeeded Augustus in power. Thus, Rome's
future prosperity itself is here associated with the
steadily waxing tree. A far mightier, but subtly related phallic image closes the ode. Speaking of Jupiter,
to whom Augustus is <u>minor</u> but <u>secundus</u>, Horace proclaims (59f.):

> tu parum castis inimica mittes
> fulmina lucis.

> You will cast your hostile
> thunderbolts into unchaste groves.

Commenting on <u>lucis</u>, Bennett designates them groves
polluted "by the vile orgies of the time." He is doubtless right, but I think we do not go astray in understanding Roman moral degeneracy in general. In any case,
groves admit symbolically of either a masculine or feminine connotation, while, if there is an ultimate phallic
emblem, it is the thunderbolt. Here its divine virile

159

force overwhelms the human, so pathetically puny by contrast, despite the evocation of unrestrained license. Now, this, though Jupiter's work, is Augustus' cause. Add that Augustus is a "second Jupiter", and we cannot escape the inference that the days of Roman profligacy are numbered. And, even as the groves smolder in ruin, Marcellus' tree steadily grows.

Jupiter, by so displaying his power, inarguably exhibits his _virtus_. In the Cleopatra ode (1:37), Augustus is made to exercise a virile potency _qua virtus_ nearly as striking. His victim is not only a woman, but pejorative womanliness--that batch of malignant impulses, that is to say, which Horace habitually attaches to the dark side of the female nature. Pyrrha is an instance of it, but in Cleopatra he offers an instance of Dionysus himself. Plotting "demented" ruin for Rome (_l_. 7), she is so drunk on sweet fortune (11f.) as to entertain any illusive hope. Similarly, her drunken wits are fraught with crazed delusions (_l_. 14). She is also a "deadly monster" (_l_. 21), accompanied by a vile and diseased retinue (_l_. 9). But, once she is confronted by Caesar at Actium, reality displaces illusion, sobriety replaces drunkness (she drinks poison, not wine, _l_. 21), vanity becomes pride and emotion gives way ironically to reason: she dies a "deliberated" death (_l_. 29). The consummate irony, then, is that this maenad is forced to become, in the end, a man, facing up with stoic calm to defeat and death (21ff.), and the agent of her fruitful metamorphosis is the brilliant and resistless emperor-to-be. He occupies the very center of the ode (16ff.):

160

> . . . ab Italia volantem
>
> remis adurgens, accipiter velut
> mollis columbas aut leporem citus
>   venator in campis nivalis
>   Haemoniae . . .

>   . . . looming close upon her with
> his oarage, even as a hawk pursues timid
> doves or a swift hunter the hare in
> Haemonia's snowy fields . . .

We detect implications of the aggressive phallus in the
figures of hawk and hunter, but even more so in
adurgens. Symbolically, its suggestion is nothing different than in the Pyrrha (1:5, 2) and Licinius (2:10, 2)
odes, except that here it attaches to Octavian's formidable virtus. Manly he is and by a manly display of
puissance he conquers utterly over the blighting fe-
male--victor and reformer in one fell stroke.

As the Valgius ode has attested, Horace turns once
more to phallic symbolism to propound the splendor of
Augustus' military conquests. Thereafter Augustus personally partakes no further in the motif of phallic
prowess, though in itself it persists powerfully, especially in the fourth book. More important, Horace altogether drops the association of phallic might with
social reform. The reason is simple enough. Such a
combination works admirably in a figure like the thunderbolt loosed into polluted groves. But it also has severe
limitations. Enduring reform requires inspired states-
manship, not might--which obvious reflection leads
straight to the daring wisdom of the Roman Odes.

Why does the person of Horace figure so prominently

in these six lyrics? The first brims over with his
presence, meanwhile offering no mention at all of any
other identifiable personage, human or divine, save
Jupiter. Then, after peeping in at the close of both
the second and third odes, the poet devotes the first
thirty-six lines solid of the fourth _sibi_ _ipsi_. As for
the last two pieces, though he makes no personal appearance as such, his searing tone imparts a tantamount
presence.

  We really get nowhere in these odes until we grasp
that their main player is the assemblage of the muses
and their key concept the gift of ordered inspiration
that the muses purvey. Both Augustus and Jupiter, as
we shall see, are stunning beneficiaries of their muni-
ficence; and whom else might Horace include in that
company if not himself, their solemnly proclaimed priest
and spokesman? His motive far transcends anything so
simple as pride in his creative achievement.[10] With his
first words, intensely personal and proud though they
are, he subordinates himself to the muses. Theirs is
the wisdom he will teach. Consequently, its glory too
is theirs. This in itself does not perhaps justify the
inordinate prominence he gives to his person, but when
we reflect that practically all of his self-advertisement
centers on his sacred relationship to the muses, we begin to see his purpose. He can speak of himself in the
same breath with Augustus and, this side of _nefas_, even
with Jupiter, because, as one uniquely chosen of the
muses, he simply ranks with their sublimest clients in
dignity. Indeed, if Jupiter and Augustus wield civilizing authority specifically because they have the muses'
counsel (3:4, 37ff.), what of the authority of Horace,

who has their most intimate counsel and care? The function of poetry was never so breathtakingly adduced.

Accordingly, when Horace, the muses' sacred spokesman, essays moral counsel, the muse's own province, in
Odi profanum vulgus he speaks with scarcely less than
absolute authority. Little wonder, then, that he
follows his own lofty introduction with a reference to
another exalted authority (5ff.):

> Regum timendorum in proprios greges,
> reges in ipsos imperium est Iovis
>   clari Giganteo triumpho,
>   cuncta supercilio moventis.

> Rule over their own flocks belongs
> to dreaded kings; rule over the kings
> themselves belongs to Jupiter, who, re-
> nowned for his conquest of the Giants,
> moves all with the nod of his brow.

It is evident that the distance here set between Jupiter
and his subject kings chimes with the transcendence over
the common folk that Horace credits to himself in the
opening stanza.[11] We have already seen that the concinnity is not idle.

Who besides our priceless poet would have thought
to follow these empyrean stanzas with a stray piece of
phallic symbolism (5f.):[12]

> Est ut viro vir latius ordinet
> arbusta sulcis . . .

> It is true that one man arrays
> trees more extensively in the furrow
> than another . . .

163

The figure seems further misplaced in that the context
concerns not landowners, but men standing for political
office. Some go down to the Campus more noble than
others in lineage, the poet continues, some better in
character, others in reputation, but:

> . . . aequa lege Necessitas
> sortitur insignis et imos;
>   omne capax movet urna nomen.

> . . . with impartial justice
> Necessity allots the destinies of
> the distinguished and the lowly;
> the roomy urn shakes the names of
> one and all.

That shaking of the urn ingeniously settles the issue
for the ambitious candidates; but all the less does the
lavish planter of vineyard-trees seem to fit their
company.

He fits the ode, however. Its subject is contentment, and, once he has disposed of the candidates for
political power, Horace devotes the poem's second half
to the question of wealth. The reference to the thriving planter serves to anticipate not only that topic,
but its symbolic texture; for here as previously in the
social diatribes the acquisitive instinct is made to
cast the shadow of the phallus. Specifically, Horace
weaves a symbolic argument in the ode's second half
associating the psychology of wealth with the sexual
drive.

First, the figure of the merchant ship struggling
through tumultuous seas is conjured up to impart the

164

obsessive quest for lucre (24ff.). The next key phallic
reference is as flamboyant as this last is veiled. Horace's text is that neither the hazards of sailing nor of
planting will vex the man who contents himself with
life's necessities. On the side of farming, such a man
will not be moved by "the tree now grumbling over the
rainfall, now the stars searing the fields, now the
cruel winters (30ff.)."

Though the focus now shifts from the woes of ac-
quiring wealth to those of possessing it, the symbolic
strategy remains the same. The _dominus_ who would
thrust a private promontory into the sea is again trot-
ted forth (30ff.) for our derision, and the poet continues:

> . . . sed Timor et Minae
> scandunt eodem quo dominus, neque
>   decedit aerata triremi et
>   post equitem sedet atra Cura.

> . . . but Fear and Menace mount
> where the master mounts, nor is black
> Care shed by the brass-bound yacht, and
> it sits behind the rider.

The sexual connotation of _scandere_ had long been
brilliantly elucidated by Catullus, who has "Mentula"
("Mr. Penis", the sobriquet of Mamurra) "mount" Helicon
in order to take the Muses by force (Cat. 94). Strictly, only the _dominus_ "mounts" here, but both yachtsman
and horseman easily qualify as phallic-aggressive sorts
as well. So, too, do _Timor_, _Minae_ and _Cura_ find a
ready place in the psychology of erotic conquest.

Lest we miss the literal point, that wealth entails

sorrows that it cannot cure, Horace duly states it next
(41ff.). He then closes with a refusal to trade his
Sabine vale for an "enviably pillared" manor in the new
style.

Horace's ethical advice to the Roman young thus
translates itself on the symbolic level to a familiar
condemnation of debased phallic appetency. Yet, we
have seen that the impulse to phallic prowess has its
glorius side as well. It is to this that the poet
turns next.

The transition to the second ode is the smoothest
within the group:

> Angustum amice pauperiem pati
> robustus acri militia puer
>   condiscat et Parthos feroces
>   vexet eques metuendus hasta . . .
>
>
>   Let the young man, toughened by
> military service, learn to endure
> straitened poverty gladly and, a horse-
> man to be dreaded for his spear, let
> him harry the fierce Parthian . . .

Condiscat reaffirms the educational intent broached at
the beginning of Odi profanum vulgus, while the exhorta-
tion that the Roman puer should learn to endure poverty
amiably carries the moral counsel of the first ode to
its ultimate conclusion. Up to a point, continuity inheres on the symbolic level as well. A sense of aggressive phallic might informs metuendus hasta no less than
it does the forerunning symbols of ship, promontory and
the like. Even more punctiliously, eques picks up
equitem, phallic connotation and all, in the previous

ode (1. 40). But the symbolic burden obviously differs. Far from corruption, the phallic suggestions evoke pristine Roman virtus.

Horace fashions the same evocation a moment later through the phallic figure of ascending flight (21ff.):

> Virtus recludens immeritis mori
> caelum, negata temptat iter via,
> coetusque vulgaris et udam
> spernit humum fugiente penna.

> Valor, unlocking the heavens for those undeserving to die, essays the journey by a path denied and scorns the common throng and the damp earth with fleeing wing.

Through the symbolism, the ascent of virtus to enduring life (and away from the profanum vulgus) is winged not only with the rising might of the phallus, but with its progenitive force as well. The debased phallic aggression configured in the first ode is thus turned utterly around, and, clearly, a tacit argument for moral reform develops turn for turn with the symbolic reversal.

Such an argument is, of course, also accessible on the literal level. With the second ode Horace completes his prescription for reinvigorated personal virtue in the young. Not surprisingly, it harks back to the values of yore, a mixture of simplicity in personal behavior and valor in the public cause that comprised the virtus antiquorum. The advantage gained by the symbolism lies in its capacity to relate both the ethical and physical aspects of virtus to natural urges that are in the process of taking form in the youthful breast. Accordingly,

<u>virtus</u> becomes a delicate blend of restraint and sublimation, a wholesome tempering of youthful <u>esprit</u>. And this spells education. Thus, it is through the symbolism that we are kept most strictly in touch with the odes' intrinsic purpose.

As we have seen, the high hopes of the second ode come tumbling down in the sixth, its positional counterpart. Both military prowess (9ff.) and moral vigor (17ff.) have wasted away, and, on the ode's direct evidence, there is no chance that the Roman <u>puer</u> will be able to restore them. This is pretty much as we have noted, but a little attention to detail, structural and symbolic, reveals depths of pessimism yet unimagined.

The poem starts with an emphatic recollection of ancestral sins, dwells on current enormities of moral behavior and ends with a despairing look at the generation yet to come. It thus places Rome in the midst of an incontrovertible tradition of vice and dereliction, even though it holds out at its start the possibility of redemption through religious reform. Of <u>hope</u> for such redemption, let it be made clear, it offers nothing.

Horace assigns the cause of Rome's moral degeneration in these sententious words (17ff.):

> Fecunda culpae saecula nuptias
> primum inquinavere et genus et domos;
>   hoc fonte derivata clades
>   in patriam populumque fluxit.

>   Generations fertile in vice first
> defiled marriage and the family and the
> home; drawn from this fount, calamity
> has overwhelmed country and populace.

It would strain the literal sense to interpret that the
defilement of marriage, family, and home has polluted
the very womb of Roman dignity and honor; but that is
precisely what the symbolism, based in hoc fonte, imparts. Nor do we feel the full brunt of it till we
grasp that the entire poem arrays itself about this
axial piece of procreative symbolism: previous generations (maiorum, l. 1; saecula, l. 17)[13] mothered (fecunda
culpae, l. 17) the pollution of marriage; from this
corrupted womb (hoc fonte) has proceeded the present
blighted generation (21ff.), which in turn will beget a
worse one still (47f.). The pessimism of the final
stanza thus cannot be mitigated by any manner of special
pleading. It is of a piece with the whole. Vice has
become Rome's heritage, bred into the very genes.

The gloom would be total but for a bit of phallic
fun toward the close. Horace has just completed his
lurid portrait of the typical Roman bride, who, with her
husband's tacit connivance, sells her sexual favors
(another aspect of the corrupted fons) to whomever. Not
the progeny of such parents were the youths who struck
down Pyrrhus, Antiochus and Hannibal, avers the poet
(37ff.),

> . . . sed rusticorum mascula militum
> proles, Sabellis docta ligonibus
>   versare glebas et severae
>   matris ad arbitrium recisos
>
> portare fustis . . .

> ° . . but the masculine offspring
> of rustic soldiers taught to turn the
> sod with Sabine hoes and to cut and

> fetch firewood at a stern mother's
> behest . . .

The boys' sexual innocence shines wholesomely through
the symbolism, and Horace drives the point home by fixing their closely supervised wood-chores (which do not
promise the high-piled hearth of Thaliarchus) at just
that hour when the lover's day dawns (41ff.):

> . . . sol ubi montium
> mutaret umbras et iuga demeret
>   bobus fatigatis, amicum
>   tempus agens abeunte curru.

>   . . . when the sun was changing
> the shadows of the mountains and re-
> moving the yoke from the weary oxen,
> ushering in the pleasant hours with
> his departing chariot.

But gloom comes to infect even the comic relief.
For if these youths, whose likes Rome will never see
again (47f.), so differ from the moderns, what is their
likeness to those Horace would call to arms in the second
ode? Nor do the hopes of Odi profanum vulgus fare a
whit better. Indeed, the behavior of the society de-
picted in the sixth ode is par excellence that of an
"uninitiate throng." And must we not be tempted to conclude that, in the end, the irredeemable corruption of
the masses devastates Horace's sacred educational mission? At the least, the evocations of the corrupted
womb here, closing a grim circle with the burden of
phallic corruption there, make a mockery of the first
ode's counsels of moderation. The result is all but impossible strains on the central lyric, Descende caelo,

if the Roman Odes are not to founder in despair.

Architecturally, the three inner odes are a carefully laid triangle, with the central panel of Descende caelo at its apex. Both the third and fifth odes, we will recall, are devoted to pieces of consilia, one delivered before the assembly of the gods, the other before the Roman senate. The main function of this construct is to point up the theme of consilium at the heart of Descende caelo. Simultaneously, as we have noted, its theme of apotheosis lends emphasis to Augustus, as at once man and god, in the same panel. We thus begin to see that this theme of itself participates in the general trend toward the center. That observation is borne out on grounds of placement: the theme is transacted exclusively in the anchoring odes, 3 and 5, thus converging from both sides upon the middle. And the terms of its execution reveal much more.

The third ode states merely that Augustus will one day imbibe nectar in heaven (11f.); but the fifth gives him a share of the Jovian thunder that rings in the ode:

> Caelo tonantem credidimus Iovem
> regnare: praesens divus habebitur
> Augustus adiectis Britannis
> imperio gravibusque Persis.

> We believe that Jupiter rules in
> heaven on the evidence of his thunder-
> ings: Augustus will be considered a god
> in our midst once the Britons and the
> dread Persians have been added to our
> rule.

171

The lines masterfully restate the theme of Augustus as
a second Jupiter. While piously reserving a distinct
and lesser domain for the emperor, they actually lay
greater stress on a like immediacy of godhead. For what
is the effect of Jupiter's thunderclap if not to make
him praesentem, a god in our midst, the very epithet
that here decorates Augustus. Horace, we will recall,
has already implicitly laid claim to a Jovian sub-
limity of his own at the start of Odi profanum vulgus.
What is the meaning of these subtle equivalencies? The
answer comes in Descende caelo, where we find that all
three are equally dependent upon a yet sublimer force,
the enlightening counsel of the muses. Hence, the
theme of apotheosis not only looks to the center, but
is there also placed in perspective and, indeed,
resolved.

Now to Descende caelo itself. Horace's purpose in
the ode's first half has never been adequately understood. Here he establishes two fundamental aspects of
his relationship with the muses, his immediate access
to their inspiration (1-8) and his trust in their
tutelary powers (9-36). Both these factors are entirely
vital to the poem's design and meaning, the first sub-
stantiating the poet's case for peerage with Jupiter and
Augustus, the second prefiguring that magnificent testament to the muses' tutelary might that dominates the
ode's second half.

At the precise midpoint Augustus comes in for the
highest praise that the poet can bestow (37ff.):

Vos Caesarem altum, militia simul
fessas cohortis abdidit oppidis,

172

> finire quaerentem labores
> Pierio recreatis antro.

> In a Pierian grotto, as he seeks
> to finish his labors, you revitalize
> great Caesar, as soon as he has set-
> tled his armies, weary with war, in
> townships.

The labors which the emperor seeks to complete cannot
but be the works of peace, preeminently, therefore, the
social reform which has found so urgent a place in the
patriotic odes. These he ponders, aided by the creative inspirations of the muses. But the setting, the
Pierian grotto, is the most significant detail of the
entire composition, for, as the sequel shows, it represents nothing less than the universal womb of harmony,
order and wisdom.

In the next breath, Horace addresses the muses as
almae, thus corroborating the implication of the womb
in _Pierio_ _antro_:

> Vos lene consilium et datis et dato
> gaudetis almae.

> You, o nurturing ones, both
> give gentle counsel and rejoice in
> gentle counsel already given.

The muses "nurture," obviously, by purveying inspiration;
thus, they nourish, or "re-create" Augustus as he ponders his program for peace.[14] We might expect Horace to
continue by enumerating the works of peace and the acts
of enlightenment that will crown them with success.

173

But this would be to abandon the strategy of concentric
structure. The center gains emphasis precisely by
isolation. Thus it is that the balance of the ode
dwells on the uses not of peace, but of violence (42ff.):

> Scimus ut impios
> Titanas immanemque turbam
>   fulmine sustulerit caduco,
>
> qui terram inertem, qui mare temperat
> ventosum, et urbes regnaque tristia
>   divosque mortalisque turmas
>   imperio regit unus aequo.
>
> Magnum illa terrorem intulerat Iovi
> fidens iuventus horrida bracchiis
>   fratresque tendentes opaco
>   Pelion imposuisse Olympo.
>
> Sed quid Typhoeus et validus Mimas,
> aut quid minaci Porphyrion statu,
>   quid Rhoetus evulsisque truncis
>   Enceladus iaculator audax
>
> Contra sonantem Palladis aegida
> possent ruentes? Hinc avidus stetit
>   Vulcanus, hinc matrona Iuno et
>   numquam umeris positurus arcum,
>
> qui rore puro Castiliae lavit
> crinis solutos, qui Lyciae tenet
>   dumeta natalemque silvam,
>   Delius et Patareus Apollo.
>
> Vis consili expers mole ruit sua:
> vim temperatam di quoque provehunt
>   in maius . . .
>
> We know how he obliterated the
> impious Titans and their monstrous horde
> with his flying thunderbolts who tempers

174

the lifeless earth and the windy sea
and governs, he alone, with impartial
rule over the cities and the gloomy
realms and the gods and the throng of
mortals. That confident crew of
youths, bristling with arms, had in-
stilled vast terror in Jupiter, as did
the brothers who strained to place
Pelion atop shady Olympus. But what
could Typhoeus or strong Mimas, or
what could Porphyrion of threatening
stature, or Rhoetus or Enceladus, that
bold slinger of uprooted trees, avail
rushing headlong against the ringing
shield of Pallas? On the one side
stood eager Vulcan, on the other the
Matron Juno and he who will never remove his bow from his shoulder, who
washes his flowing locks in the pure
dew of Castalia, who abides in Lycian
thickets and the forest of his birthplace, Apollo of Delos and Patera.
Force without counsel collapses of its
own weight: tempered force the gods
even increase . . .

It is the logic of the ode that these brutes and
brigands who threatened Olympus are as they are because
they know not the muse. Vis consili expers is their
style, and the lene consilium which they lack is the
gift of the muses. On the other hand, "moderated
force"--force moderated by consilium--is pure Pierian.
Though unnamed, in fact, the muses are everywhere in
these verses. First, they reside in the verb tempero,
which brackets the passage (45, 66). The word is a
musical term meaning to "tune" or "modulate". Thus, in
"tempering" land and sea, Jupiter exercises a function
of the muses. Similarly, to "govern with impartial

rule" gods and men, cities and the underworld is to
harmonize the entire universe. Jupiter, therefore, is
the celestial paradigm of that _vis temperata_ which,
when practiced by mankind, reaps divine rewards.

Then a bold Horatian surprise. Having so provided
the father of the gods with every faculty to turn back
violent assault, the poet suddenly strips him bare.
Jupiter was sorely frightened prior to the fray, we are
told. The explanation once again rests in the role of
the muses. Horace had spent virtually the entire first
half of the ode establishing his own trust in their
protection. They had made him _animosus_ even as an in-
fant (_l_. 20); they had saved his life at Philippi and
elsewhere (25ff.) and, given their company, he is ready
to face any danger (29ff.). Jupiter, however, is not.[15]
Momentarily at least his trust in the strength of enlightenment deserts him, and the lapse of faith leaves
him vulnerable. How more stunningly could Horace have
driven home the ode's key premise, that none but the
almae Musae exercise the most sublime of divine offices?
He proceeds to underscore the point even more firmly by
ennobling two deities preeminent for their possession
of _consilium_ (_i.e._, the grace of the muses), Athena and
Apollo. Far from terrified, they, and especially the
god of the lyre, are limned in attitudes of serene self-
confidence. The precise reason we learn moments later:
vis sine consilio mole ruit sua. Their museless adver-
saries simply stand no chance against their superior
enlightenment. Nor need we fret greatly over the
affrighted Jupiter, for he is not so much supplanted as
refined in the figure of Apollo, who in the attributes
of bow and Castilian fount demonstrates the same quali-

ties of _vis_ and temperance that predicated his father
earlier on.

There is evident allegory in all of this. In
Jupiter and Apollo we see Augustus, who, likewise
nourished with the civilizing inspiration of the muses,
has withstood and will withstand again every brute
counterforce. The more signal inference, however, is
that, like the all-governing gods, the emperor wields a
power, gentled by counsel, that instills and maintains
a tempered harmony and order. Success, therefore, not
alone in war, but also in the tasks of peace is firmly
assured by his possession of the muses' gifts.

It is important to note the sharp departure from
the norm in the ode's central imagery. Nowhere in Horace does the feminine in nature accede to such honor as
in this axial panel. We are not surprised to find the
faculty of inspiration represented as a feminine quan-
tity. This had been associated with the muses from
time out of mind. But the association of reasoned
counsel with the feminine impinges upon a similarly
aboriginal male preserve. We perhaps see the trans-
ference at its clearest when we grasp that Horace all
but blends the muses and Apollo into one sublime force,
down even to the implication of an oracular function
for the _almae_ _Musae_. For what is the purveying of
civilizing counsel if not an ideal enactment of the
prophetic function? And witness the god himself. Far
from Musagetes, leader of the muses, he is their partner at best. He prevails only because he has their
grace of _consilium_, which is itself _lene_, "gentle",
"mild"--quintessentially feminine. And so is the god's
own description. He is masculine enough in that he

will never remove his bow from his shoulder, but, preening himself in her sacral waters, he resembles nothing so much as one of the indwelling nymphs of Castalia. More spectacular, of course, is Jupiter's dependence upon the feminine. He remains _princeps_ of the universe, but he accedes to that dignity only after accession to the muses' grace. The moral for Augustus is unmistakable, but, equally important, the vindication of the female principle is entire.

It is a nice irony that, with the notion of a _vis temperata_, Horace also feminizes and refines his concept of _virtus_--manliness. In this regard, he has hitherto been content to recommend a mixture of valor and simplicity for his youthful audience. I do not suggest that he now alters that prescription. Indeed, coming as a _consilium_ of a high priest of the muses, it is inspired, inviolable. But such _virtus_ is for every Roman. Now he adumbrates a _virtus_ of leadership wherein civilized enlightenment holds such sway that reason and force, mind and body, the lyre and the bow are blended into an irresistible harmonium. Apollo is its celestial paradigm, Augustus its terrestrial embodiment. Its result is culture in the amplest sense, a realized world harmony and order. But as it is in the last analysis the _almae Musae_ who temper force, this refined _virtus_ is nothing other than _vis_ gentled and enlightened by the civilizing feminine virtues. Likewise, the muses are the fount of its harmonizing powers; and, lest we forget, it is the poet who drinks first at the muses' fount.

Horace's symbolic muse is meanwhile busily engaged in establishing a sexual grounding for the theme of mindless violence. He compresses the entire representation of close combat between gods and insurgents into a confrontation between Enceladus with his tree-trunk missiles and the impregnable shield of Athena. On the symbolic level, the vignette says that against true virtue even the most wantonly insane phallic assault proves absurdly impotent: vis consili expers mole ruit sua. The sexual grounding of such violence then becomes patent in the close, where three new wantons, Orion, Tityus and Perithous, are added to the rolls of the god-hated--all three of them sexual assailants.

Let us now take a profile of the cardinal symbolic effects in the Roman Odes. At beginning and end, first through male, then through female symbolic imagery, varying forms of excess are brought into such relief as to posit an incurable social corruption. But at the center stand the almae Musae, inspirational forces of enlightenment that mother universal order. If the symbolism thus swells both Horace's most pessimistic and optimistic accents, it does not leave quite the stand-off that obtains on the literal level. For it is now evident that the optimism at the center outweighs the peripheral despair not only by virtue of the ensemble's concentric design, nor merely because it is in the muses, his own most intimate divinities, that Horace places his trust. Rather, through the symbolism, the center has been transformed into a veritable omphalos, sacred, benign and inexhaustible, of every civilizing virtue, human and divine. We earlier remarked that Augustus could hardly fail in his labors of peace after imbibing the muses' counsel. Now his success is palpably more certain.

Finally, we may now also draw a clearer profile of the ensemble's literal texture. It has become gradually evident that all six odes are built upon the theme of consilium, comprising essentially a set of advisements which Horace as sacerdos Musarum explicates with a view to Rome's welfare. First come his counsels of virtus to the young, last his counsel, however negatively shaded, to repair the ruins of sacred and familial institutions. Inwardly, two great "historical" instances of consilia keyed to the preservation of the state bracket a central appeal to the preserving consilium of the muses. And, again, the poet's hopes outweigh his fears.

We will recall, however, that Horace's pessimism resurfaces toward the close of the third book in a last, despairing look at the society's benighted youth. The effect is to revive the old ambivalence regarding Rome's future once and for all. The poet indeed trusts that, with the inspiration of the muses, the emperor will restore the ancient Roman virtues. Yet, he harbors an equally strong faith in the capacity of social excess to perpetuate itself indefinitely. He indicates as much in the final verses of the same ode (3:24, 62ff.). Wealth piles up, he laments, but it somehow never suffices the wealthy. We have learned enough about the implications of avarice to understand that, until it is renounced, Rome's social corruption will never heal over. But avarice feeds perpetually upon itself,[16] as does society's sickness.

Thus, though the first three books disclose no clear confidence in Rome's future, we may have encountered something even more valuable. Unless I am badly mistaken, we have found in Horace a passionate, yet

180

objective and strikingly independent political judgment.
The last quality is particularly arresting. Throughout
the patriotic odes of the first three books there are
simply no traces of a compulsion to please imperial
ears. We encounter plenteous praise for the emperor, to
be sure, but nothing obsequious. Meanwhile, ultimate
honor is reserved for the muses and devolves thence inevitably upon their priest, ward and principal exponent,
Q. Horatius Flaccus, poet and private gentleman.

This complexion of things alters radically in the
patriotic odes of the fourth book. Praise of Augustus
is pervasive, unrestrained and, to those of us at least
who would subscribe to Nabokov's dictum that portraits
of heads of state ought not to exceed the size of a
postage stamp, dismaying. Simultaneously, the muses,
though honored and defended, are demoted. No longer
are they the fount of civilizing order, wisdom and harmony. That distinction falls to the emperor. Perforce,
the poet also accepts a demotion, at times even
acquiescing, as Fraenkel nicely perceives,[17] to blend
his hallelujahs in with the voice of the masses.

It is precisely here that we engage the single
most startling departure from the political perspective
of the first three books. What has become of the
profanum vulgus? All of the poet's profound doubts concerning the redeemability of Roman society vanish without a trace in the fourth book and, alas, without explanation. Instead, as we shall see, we are served with
one insouciant contradiction after another, among them
this crucial specimen. At 3:24, 35f., Horace exclaims,
"What is the good of empty laws if custom is dead?"
Ten years later he can publish (4:5, 22), "Custom and

181

law have overcome the pollution of crime." History does
not attest to a genuine revival of custom between 23 and
13 B.C., nor, I submit, would the Horace of 23 B.C. have
subscribed to such a proposition in 13 B.C.

Horace's critics have made no issue of the drasti-
cally altered political bias of the last book. Most
have not recognized it. Commager does, but his explanation is sheer sentimentality: "The Golden Age was no
longer a fitful dream, but a refulgent reality, and one
could only be quietly grateful to the man who had
created it."[18] Before we attempt a more cogent explanation, however, it behooves us to see how golden indeed
Horace limns the "new" age.

The old virtues, we are told, are completely restored (4:15), with vice (4:5; 4:15), including female
license (4:5) overcome. The younger generation is
brilliant beyond all expectation (4:4; 4:14). Military
prowess has recovered its full vigor (4:4; 4:5; 4:14;
4:15), peace reigns (4:5; 4:15), agriculture flourishes
(4:5; 4:15) and Rome is saved from violence both from
within (4:15) and without (4:5; 4:15). Of all these
blessings only the very last was vouchsafed in Books I-
III, whereas the only vice there emphasized that has
not been explicitly eradicated is avarice. Neither does
the poet make an issue of it, however--avarice, his old
bête noire! What has wrought this miracle of recovery?
If the cause is reducible to a single factor, it is
Augusti paternus animus (4:4, 26f.).

The fourth ode tells the main tale of the patriotic
odes of the last book. Augustus there stands forth as
the educational model from which the triumphant virtus
of Drusus and Tiberius, and, hence, the enlightened

future leadership of Rome, derives. The ode is thus an elaboration of the promise of Descende caelo, but conspicuously without the services of Pieria. Augustus, not the muses, is the sublime educator, and the seminal inspiration which he provides, while indeed almus, is strictly paternal. So far are the almae Musae left behind.

Throughout the fresh set of patriotic odes Horace's renewed masculine bias is duly reflected in the symbolism, which is almost without exception phallic. Though not particularly widespread, it tends to the monumental in scale and the dynamic in execution. At its peak, indeed, it becomes an extravaganza, a very revel, of phallic prowess.

The peak comes in the selfsame fourth ode, Qualem ministrum. The ode begins with an immense epic period that compares the freshly victorious Drusus first to an eagle and then to a lion. We watch the eagle, impelled by patrius vigor, proceed through various stages of growth culminating in victorious combat with doughty serpents:

> Qualem ministrum fulminis alitem,
> cui rex deorum regnum in avis vagas
> permisit expertus fidelem
> Iuppiter in Ganymede flavo,
>
> olim iuventas et patrius vigor
> nido laborum protulit inscium,
> vernique iam nimbis remotis
> insolitos docuere nisus
>
> venti paventem, mox in ovilia
> demisit hostem vividus impetus,
> nunc in reluctantis dracones
> egit amor dapis atque pugnae . . .

> Like the winged agent of light-
> ening, to whom Jupiter, king of the
> gods, gave dominion over the wander-
> ing birds, having found him loyal in
> the affair of golden-haired Ganymede,
> whom youth and his father's vigor first
> usher forth, all unused to toil, from
> the nest and, despite his timidity, the
> spring gales then train to unwonted
> efforts in the distant clouds and whom
> the lively spirit of attack soon sets
> down in hostile assault upon the sheep-
> folds and lust for prey and battle
> finally drives against fiercely-resist-
> ing serpents . . .

All of the ode's main effects build upon this robust
simile of the eagle. The figure's most evident purpose
is to show that, like the eagle, Drusus has waxed strong
to overcome the Vindelici (17ff.). Meanwhile, a further
typical suggestion crops up. Because of its proven
loyalty, Jupiter has granted the eagle rule over the
whole winged kind (2f.). Seeing that the eagle represents Drusus, who was in fact Augustus' stepson and
favorite, this seeming poetic trifle reveals something
about the youth's imperial prospects. The last such
figure we encountered was Marcellus. More accurately,
we encountered a growing tree. It seems hardly accidental that we are here presented with a growing eagle.

The similes also share an intrinsic phallic symbolism. With Drusus we are made to focus on the
specific quality of growing military prowess. Now,
growth, as we shall see, is the leitmotif of Qualem
ministrum, and in Horatian symbolism that notion by itself suffices to intimate the tumescent phallus. But
so, too, is the eagle a phallic symbol. The eagle's

growth to soaring domination thus symbolically represents a gradual, yet inevitable realization of phallic
prowess. Such, by analogy, has been Drusus' rise to
virtus.

But, to say the least, virtus so qualified falls
short of the ideal, for it lacks the refinement of mens,
or, in the terms of Descende caelo, of consilium. What
is missing, in short, is the perfecting ingredient of
growth, education. Here the term patrius vigor (l. 5)
subtly makes itself felt. Though in itself suggesting
nothing beyond inherited virile might, it paves the way
through its citation of effective paternal influence
for the key service of Augustus, the paternus animus
(27f.), in shaping Drusus' mind and character.

One further detail of the eagle motif deserves
notice. In subduing reluctantis dracones, the sky-
phallus overcomes the formidably phallic guardians of
earth. Accordingly, the male principle triumphs over
the female.[19] The upshot will become clear presently.

Next we are shown what the Vindelici witnessed
(22ff.):

> . . . sed diu
> lateque victrices catervae
> consiliis iuvenis revictae
>
> sensere, quid mens rite, quid indoles
> nutrita faustis sub penetralibus
> posset, quid Augusti paternus
> in pueros animus Nerones.
>
> . . . but their hordes, victorious
> far and wide and now conquered in turn
> by the counsels of a youth, learned what
> it is that intelligence and character

185

> nurtured fitly beneath an auspicious
> roof could accomplish and what the
> paternal mind of Augustus could do
> for the youthful Neros.

We note particularly how the words <u>consiliis</u>, <u>mens</u>,
<u>nutrita</u>, <u>animus</u> reflect the great central themes of
<u>Descende</u> <u>caelo</u>. Drusus, however, has been nourished
with intellect and judgment not by any muse, but by
Augustus, the inspirational paternal mind, the consummate educator.

The poet now briefly reverts to analogy with the
animal world to press home his emphasis on paternity.
Strong creatures, he declares are created by strong and
good: in good horses resides <u>patrum</u> <u>virtus</u>. And then,
appropos of humans (33ff.),

> . . . doctrina sed vim promovet insitam,
> rectique cultus pectora roborant;
> utcumque defecere mores,
> indecorant bene nata culpae.

> . . . but teaching refines inborn
> might, and training in rectitude
> strengthens the breast; wherever char-
> acter falls short, vice degrades the
> well-born.

After this stress on enlightened <u>vis</u> there can remain
scant doubt that Horace has quietly set out to amend
the terms of <u>Descende</u> <u>caelo</u> in favor of the male principle and its living quintessence, the emperor.

Nor is he yet nearly finished with the male principle. Still keeping to the motif of growth, he lets
his gaze fall on Rome--all of Rome, past, present and

future--and in a bravura display of symbolic utterance
pronounces the fatherland an unweariable wonder of
virile might.

He works up to his symbolic extravaganza with a
cunningly matched pair of phallic effects, the one
(crevit, l. 46) lulling us with the leitmotif before
the other (rectos, l. 48), given the context, primes us
for audacities to come. Suddenly then we are listening
to Hannibal as he extolls Rome's irrepressible virtus
(53ff.):

> Gens, quae cremato fortis ab Ilio
> iactata Tuscis aequoribus sacra
> natosque maturosque patres
> pertulit Ausonias ad urbis,
>
> duris ut ilex tonsa bipennibus
> nigrae feraci frondis in Algido,
> per damna, per caedis, ab ipso
> ducit opes animumque ferro.
>
> Non hydra secto corpore firmior
> vinci dolentem crevit in Herculem,
> monstrumve submisere Colchi
> maius Echioniaeve Thebae.
>
> Merses profundo: pulchrior evenit:
> luctere: multa proruet integrum
> cum laude victorem geretque
> proelia coniugibus loquenda.
>
>
> Stout enough after the burning of
> Ilium to convey its rites, though tossed
> by Etruscan seas, its children and aged
> fathers to Ausonian cities, that people,
> like the oak shorn by the hard axe in
> Algidus, rich in dark frondage, draws
> strength and life from the cruel lopping
> itself, from the very steel. The hydra,

its body slashed, does not grow more
firm to assail Hercules, who mourns
defeat, nor have the Colchians reared
a monster more huge nor Echionian
Thebes. Plunge it into the deep: it
emerges more beautiful; wrestle with
it: amidst great praise it will throw
its opponent, though he has never known
defeat before, and it will wage battles
for wives to tell of.

Horace, as we have seen, was not above casting himself
in the role of the phallus; now he extends the distinction to Rome. The intended effect is not nearly so
droll as in that earlier ode, however. Comedy inheres
inevitably--enough to dissociate the poet of the _levis_
camena from too much epic solemnity--but it is far
overriden by an earnest, resolving emphasis on the
leitmotif of surging, virile growth. Thus, Rome's prowess is what it always was and, the more thanks to
Augustus, always will be.

How does Augustus figure so vitally? Lest we miss
the reasoning, Horace injects its premise in his parting words (73ff.):

Nil Claudiae non perficiunt manus,
quas et benigno numine Iuppiter
    defendit et curae sagaces
        expediunt per acuta belli.

There is nothing that Claudian
might does not accomplish, which Jupiter with his kindly will defends and
keen counsel speeds through the dangers
of war.

Though the passage concerns only military success, its

188

terms range far wider. Manus denotes physical, curae
sagaces mental vis, and the Neros possess both. The
first derives merely from their being Roman, but on the
ode's testimony it is Augustus who, through his doctrina,
provides Drusus with the latter. Since, in turn, Drusus
represents Rome's future, the ode's final import is most
reassuring. Augustus has succeeded in transmitting the
best of the ancestral tradition intact to the younger
generation. The emperor having thus himself effectively
redeemed her young, Rome is assured the irrepressible
vitality to which Hannibal testifies for time to come.
Hence, the question of her future prosperity, left in
suspense over the first three books, is quite resolved.

Qualem ministrum was one of the two compositions
expressly ordered by the emperor to honor his stepsons,
Drusus and Tiberius. Quae cura parentum (4:14) is the
other. Aside from the fact that the latter is addressed
specifically to Augustus and so opens with an outpour-
ing of his praises, the two are remarkably similar in
structure. The first part of Quae cura parentum cul-
minates in a pair of epic similes honoring Tiberius, a
bridge portion attributes fundamental responsibility for
his success to the emperor and the close celebrates the
respect won from Rome's enemies under Augustus' sway.
The execution, however, does not measure up to the high
style of Qualem ministrum. Witness the bridge passage
(33f.). Horace assigns the main credit for Tiberius'
victory over the Raeti to Augustus because it was won
with his "troops, counsel and gods." Only the detail of
counsel manages to sound an essential chord, but,
trapped as it is between the ludicrous and the contrived,
it accomplishes virtually nothing.

189

Hence, Tiberius fails to reap nearly the benefits
of the Horatian muse that fell to Drusus in the fourth
ode. Indeed, here is one of the few instances in the
Odes where Horace may be said to have strained his art,
his symbolic art included, too far. We break in on an
epic simile honoring Tiberius' martial magnificence
(17ff.):

> . . . spectandus in certamine Martio,
> devota morti pectora liberae
>   quantis fatigaret ruinis,
>   indomitas prope qualis undas
>
> exercet Auster, Pleiadum choro
> scindente nubes, impiger hostium
>   vexare turmas et frementem
>   mittere equum medios per ignis.
>
> Sic tauriformis volvitur Aufidus,
> qui regna Dauni praefluit Apuli
>   cum saevit horrendamque cultis
>   diluviem meditatur agris,
>
> ut barbarorum Claudius agmina
> ferrata vasto diruit impetu
>   primosque et extremos metendo
>   stravit humum sine clade victor . . .

> . . . a marvel to behold in martial
> conflict for the devastation with which
> he wasted breasts devoted to a free man's
> death, rather like Auster when, the chorus
> of the Pleiades parting the clouds, it
> harries the indomitable waves, tireless to
> vex the enemy squadrons and to send his
> horse roaring through the flame's midst.
> So rolls bull-formed Aufidus, which flows
> through the Apulian realms of Daunus, when
> it rages and devises horrendous flood for
> the tilled fields as does Claudius when he

> cleaves the mail-clad lines of the
> barbarians and, by mowing down the
> first and the last, victoriously
> strews the earth without casualty
> to his own . . .

The passage is not without its grace. The confused
swirl of its images turns itself to account by mimicking
the whirligig of war; and the subtle citation of the
four elements lends tone to the epic ambience. Some
aspects of the sexual symbolism are also finely wrought.
Both the virile image of reaping and the hints of female subjugation that cling to the harrassment of sea
and field are up to the usual Horatian standard. So too
the phallic implication of the plunging steed. But the
use of storm winds to symbolize masculine sexual prow-
ess--which suggestion it must carry to keep the tableau
in balance--is unconvincing; and by masculinizing the
Aufidus Horace reverses the symbolic value he normally
assigns to water.[20] The only radical flaw, however, is
the unfortunate prope qualis. It evidently occurs as a
concession to logic. Wind cannot ruin waves as Tiberius
ruins the foe. Hence the qualification "rather like,"
which ruins the simile.

The remainder of the ode goes more felicitiously,
as henceforth the expression of virile conquest is
assigned to its resultant effect, female submission.
First, addressing Augustus and citing his Egyptian conquest (35f.), Horace speaks of that happy day when,

> portus Alexandrea supplex
> et vacuam patefecit aulam . . .

the Alexandrian port became your

> suppliant and laid open its vacant
> palace to you . . .

Later on (45ff.), he identifies a series of subjugated--
or, in some instances, merely mollified--enemies by their
principal rivers. Here the water imagery reverts to its
ordinary sexual intimation. Underscoring the femininity
of it all, the poet alludes to the Nile in most demure
symbolic terms as a river _fontium_ _qui_ _celat_ _origines_--
"which conceals its wellsprings." We note the artful
contrast of _celat_ with _patefecit_ in line 36. Then, as
so often, Horace complements a citation of waters with
a reference to earth (_l_. 50), again sounding the theme
of female subjugation.

One noteworthy grace of this close (34-52) is the
antithesis it cuts with the ending of _Qualem_ _ministrum_,
its companion piece. Both passages honor Roman _virtus_
in phallic terms but, by laying emphasis here on the
female quarry, Horace neatly avoids repeating the stark
masculine accents of the earlier close.

The following (and final) ode, however, witnesses
one last phallic flourish in the style of _Qualem_
ministrum. Horace is commending the emperor for his
restoration of those ancient ways (13ff.),

> . . . per quas Latinum nomen et Italae
> crevere vires, famaque et imperi
> porrecta maiestas ad ortus
> solis ab Hesperio cubili.

> . . . through which the Latin
> name and Italian might grew and the
> fame and grandeur of empire was stretched
> to the rising sun from its western bed.

The lines sketch not only Rome's territorial expansion,
but her growth over the course of time (adumbrated in
the sequence Latinum, Italae, imperii) from the city's
inception to Horace's own day. On the symbolic level
the words crevere porrecta and, in its root sense,
maiestas plainly declare that the terms of growth are
phallic. Clearly, too, the verses enlarge upon the
close of Qualem ministrum. That passage, while extolling
the same virtues that Horace now pronounces restored had
celebrated Rome's capacity to surge up in indomitable
bloom in the very throes of destruction. It has now
bloomed once more and grown to unprecedented dimensions.
Again, therefore, Rome is what it always was, only more
so--again distinctly without that inspiration of the
almae Musae once deemed indispensable.

Dive quem proles (4:6) proves yet another companion
piece to Qualem ministrum, in some respects the most
instructive of all. In form a hymn to Apollo, the ode
celebrates both the god's bow and his lyre, invoking him
as Horace's own patron god in the latter function and
proceeding thence to an imaginary rehearsal of the newly
composed Carmen Saeculare under the poet's own direction.[21] The ode's unity, less than apparent at first
glance, is best apprehended through its reminiscences
of Descende caelo and the Roman Odes in general.

The reminiscences are at least four: the themes of
vis consili expers and civilized inspiration from
Descende caelo; the theme of divine favor for Rome from
3:3 and the theme of the poet's educational function
from 3:1. The central portrait of Apollo, we may note,
also derives from Descende caelo. There the god of the
lyre washed his locks in the Castalian fount as here

(1. 26) in the Xanthus; and Horace's assertion there
that the god "will never move his bow from his shoulder"
is amply borne out in the present ode. As in Qualem
ministrum, however, the reminiscences serve essentially
to contradict their models.

We start with Apollo as Rome's savior from, somewhat surprisingly, Achilles. There is symbolic interest
in the manner of the great warrior's fall (9ff.):

> Ille, mordaci, velut icta ferro
> pinus aut impulsa cupressus Euro,
> procidit late posuitque collum in
>   pulvere Teucro.

> He, like a pine struck by the
> biting steel or a cypress assailed
> by Eurus, sprawled far and wide and
> laid his neck in the Trojan dust.

On the one side, the felled pine contrasts with the
hewn ilex of Qualem ministrum, ironically so, since
the fallen Achilles will never rise again. On another,
it is made to recall Enceladus with his uprooted boles
in Descende caelo, for, as Horace depicts him, the
Phthian wields a vis equally devoid of consilium. No
stratagem of a wooden horse for him, avers the poet
(17ff.),

> . . . sed palam captis gravis, heu nefas! heu!
> nescios fari pueros Achivis
> ureret flammis, etiam latentem
>   matris in alvo . . .

> . . . but, openly cruel to his
> captives, alas and alack, he would

> have burned infant children in
> Achaean fires, even the child
> hidden in its mother's womb . . .

So would it have been, Horace continues, had not Apollo
and Venus prevailed upon Jupiter to favor the fortunes
of Aeneas. In short, Apollo has lene consilium,
Achilles has not, and even as god of the bow it is this
possession of civilized counsel that assures Phoebus
his victory.

So far, Horace has hewn close to the central pre-
cepts of the Roman Odes, but he next admits a deviation
typical of the fourth book. Not the muses, but their
leader, Apollo Musagetes, obtains the roles of teacher
(l. 25) and inspirator (l. 29) that Descende caelo had
made so crucial to civilized life. Though the qualification of Descende caelo is not yet so drastic as in
Qualem ministrum, one fundamental result, the promotion
of the male principle at the expense of the female, is
identical.[22]

The major flight from the Roman Odes comes with
the poet's presentation of himself as a chorus master
(31ff.). The passage shows a brilliant weave. As
Apollo teaches the muses, so Horace instructs his own
charges in lyric measure; and in so teaching these maids
and youths he performs a civilized act of benevolence
that stands in profound antithesis to Achilles' putative
savagery toward the young. We cannot begrudge the poet
this evident show of pride in his new fame. It is the
retreat from the sublime educational aims of Odi
profanum vulgus that lets us down. There he would
ennoble an entire culture by educating the minds of the

young to the holy power of music. Here he contents himself with communicating to a select band of youths a
sort of new national anthem. The philosopher king has
become the king's philosopher.

We have already found one reason why he was able
to do so. He was flattered with his new public distinction. Fraenkel points out that in _Dive_ _quem_ _proles_
alone does Horace mention his own name, and that as a
proud signature at the very close. He had become Rome's
poet laureate, and in the patriotic odes of the fourth
book he acted the part.

Still, there are strategically placed hints of
discomfort, even misgiving, in his new role. The
Censorinus ode stands at the heart of the fourth book
and draws further attention by being dressed in a meter
shared by only the first and last pieces of the original
collection. Its message, which, incidentally, appears
here for the first time in the _Odes_, is that only the
muse can bestow immortality upon men worthy of praise
and, more, only the muse bestows divinity. Obviously,
Horace is commenting on his own services to the emperor
in the fourth book.[23] Now, for the fourth book, such a
show of independence is quite exceptional. Why was Horace moved to make it? The ode itself, I think, declares
the answer. It was the _virtus_ _et_ _favor_ _et_ _lingua_
potentum _vatum_, the poet asserts, that translated Aeacus
to the isles of the blest (25ff.). _Favor_ is the key
word. Horace is aware that he owes his new eminence
largely to the favor of Augustus. Now he wants it
understood that the emperor is not alone _potens_ to bestow grace.

Nor is this the end of it. Independence verges

196

onto something like defiance once we divine the full
context of the eighth ode. Fraenkel shows the way by
demonstrating that the three central odes form a distinct unit. Diffugere nives leaves us with the thought
that we are all dust and ashes; the Censorinus ode then
qualifies that sentiment by asserting the poet's power
to immortalize; and then Horace proceeds to prove his
point in Ne forte credas by immortalizing Lollius.
"This central triad, firmly linked together, is kept
separate from the poems which precede it and from those
that follow it," declares Fraenkel.[24] There, for our
purposes, he lets the matter drop. Commager adds
valuable perspective in finding that the claims for
poetry are even fiercer in Ne forte credas than in the
Censorinus ode.[25] There he contented himself with
claiming the poet's power to immortalize; here (26ff.)
he makes the stronger assertion that all who lack their
"sacred bard" are doomed to oblivion.

But why Lollius? Both Fraenkel and Commager admit
disappointment with the poet's encomium. "A list of
conventional virtues," says Commager, which he finds
"more determined than enthusiastic." Determined it is
indeed. Lollius was responsible for one of the two
greatest military debacles during Augustus' reign.
Drusus and Tiberius, or so the emperor wished the world
to believe, brought off two of its most significant
victories. Horace, as we have seen, complied with the
emperor's wish to extoll the latter. Now he is evidently
bent on demonstrating that the poet, who alone may bestow
the mantle of immortality, can bestow it, if he wishes,
even upon a loser.[26]

One would like to applaud this gesture of autonomy.

But the truth is that the poet does his cause more harm
than good by allowing it to surface. Horace's effective independence has been forfeited beyond recall by
the time his reader reaches the center of the fourth
book. Nor is it conspicuous thereafter. These remonstrations thus serve merely to remind us anew of
genuine heights of poetic sovereignty that are no more.
Yet, in a way, the gesture is reassuring. It shows
that we are not amiss in questioning the uses to which
Horace puts his patriotic muse in the fourth book. He
evidently questioned them himself.

It also shows that we must range further than our
first finding, Horace's pleasure in his new distinction,
if we are to explain his tame contentment, all in all,
to play the part of the emperor's patriot. We may start
by acknowledging that, thus far, we have stressed his
Augustanism at the expense of his patriotism. But in
truth the most salient feature of these odes is the
serene benevolence of their patriotic vision. In Horace's eyes, Rome has become all that she possibly can
be and a good bit more. The credit for her new wholeness, we have seen, goes to Augustus, but not without
evident qualms. It would, therefore, be well to inquire
whether the poet's overriding commitment might not have
been to the vision of wholeness itself and, if so, how
so.

The fourth book reverses the earlier three not on
political grounds alone. On the personal level, we
have found it brooding and dejected, even tinged with
despair as thoughts of life lose ground to a growing
thought of death. It is not uncommon for a man in such
circumstances, even one without our poet's exquisite

attachment to life, not to mention his bleak eschatology, to strengthen his identification with the community. This, I suggest, is the course that Horace took, or, more likely, the course that seduced him from a dwindling trust in his self-sufficiency. It is not accidental that the fourth book contains nothing like the claim of a unique superiority to circumstances that floats through Tyrrhena regum progenies. The circumstance of mortality had proved a piercing exception. The Horace of the fourth book is sick with mortality and, self-isolation being in such straits the least remedy, he made his peace with the community. His appointment to compose the Carmen Saeculare doubtless encouraged the decision, but the real instigation lay deeper. In the community was life. Little wonder if he pronounces it sound beyond recognition.

Seen from the Freudian perspective, the symbolism of the fourth book fortifies these conjectures significantly. It is plain that throughout the Odes Horace places enormous emphasis, both open and tacit, on the blessings of sexual vitality and, conversely, on the horrors of its loss. But the Horace of the fourth book has by admission seen the best of his own sexual vigor. To the unconscious mind, this is tantamount to the loss of the phallus. Meanwhile, the state's vigor, which the same book configures in unprecedentedly robust phallic terms, burgeons without limit. It is difficult not to infer that Horace unconsciously made good his own sexual losses in the state's access of virile majesty.

If the poet's motives were indeed as I suppose, we can more easily tolerate his numerous compromises in the patriotic odes of the last book. The abandonment

199

of his erstwhile critical rigor comes to be understood
as a psychological imperative and, thus, even his beati-
fication of Augustus is rendered less painful. Into
the bargain, we must confess that such faults would
scarcely be noticeable had not Horace himself set the
brilliant standards against which to measure them.

But nothing compensates for the demotion of the
muses.

CHAPTER SIX
THE MAKING OF MUSIC

With the great omphalic image at the center of
Descende caelo we have gotten a first taste of sexual
symbolism employed in the service of the procreative
function. Since this happens also to offer the most
significant and powerful such example, the rest is
bound to seem anticlimactic. Still, there remains considerably more of the same, some of it as aptly wrought
as anything in Horace's symbolic repertoire, and,
happily, it all finds him well within his natural element and, therefore, quite agreeably expansive.

We may start with the pious tour of his Sabine retreat which the poet conducts in the third book. The
Faunus ode finds him welcoming the wild woodland god to
his own festival, not without trepidation (3:18, 1ff.):

> Faune, Nympharum fugientum amator,
> per meos finis et aprica rura
> lenis incedas abeasque parvis
>   aequus alumnis . . .

>   Faunus, lover of fleeing nymphs,
> gently enter my boundaries and sunny
> acres and withdraw with temperate re-
> gard for my young nurslings . . .

The way in which the imagery of entry and withdrawal
supports the initial stress on the god's wantonness is
not lost upon us. Neither is the later imagery (1. 14)
where the forest is said to have shed its leaves in
honor of his arrival. Faunus is a great and formidable
phallic presence. Granted, this has nothing directly
to do with our present subject, the springs of poetic
creativity; but the two remaining stops on the poet's
tour will adequately reveal its relevance.

At 3:22 he invokes Diana in his briefest and most
neglected masterpiece:

> Montium custos nemorumque, Virgo,
> quae laborantis utero puellas
> ter vocata audis adimisque leto,
> diva triformis,
>
> imminens villae tua pinus esto,
> quam per exactos ego laetus annos
> verris obliquum meditantis ictum
> sanguine donem.

> Guardian of mountains and groves,
> Virgin, who, thrice-called, attend to
> girls laboring in childbirth and res-
> cue them from death, triform goddess,
> let this pine which looms over my
> farmhouse be yours, to which I will
> gladly give at each year's end the
> blood of a boar still practicing its
> slanting stroke.

In the Faunus ode Horace promises the sacrifice of a
kid (1. 5), if only the god will be propitious. Here
the young (meditantis gives the clue) boar serves an
analagous purpose, with the difference that the descrip-

tion of its style of attack enters graphically into the
ode's phallic dynamics. The central phallic image is,
of course, the pine. In looming over the villa, symbolically its feminine counterpart, it cuts a familiar
figure of male domination. The concert of the phallic
images is acutely powerful: the boar's blood nourish-
ing the vaunting growth of the pine. Once more, then,
an imposing symbolic presence.

Beyond this point, however, we enter territory
foreign to the Faunus ode. The great virgin goddess is
the presiding power in this lyric. Both as guardian
of groves and as an agent of fertility she is to take
the pine into her keeping. We may suppose that the
tree's hardihood, literal and emblematic, will be the
better for it, and we will not be amiss in associating
the tree with Horace himself.

But neither is this our main interest. We have,
however, reached a point where the male and female principles strike a rough balance within an ambience of fertility, which readies us for a series of odes decidedly
on our topic, starting with O fons Bandusiae (3:13):

O fons Bandusiae splendidior vitro
dulci digne mero non sine floribus,
    cras donaberis haedo,
       cui frons turgida cornibus

primis et venerem et proelia destinat;
frustra: nam gelidos inficiet tibi
    rubro sanguine rivos
       lascivi suboles gregis.

Te flagrantis atrox hora Caniculae
nescit tangere, tu frigus amabile
    fessis vomere tauris
       praebes et pecori vago.

> Fies nobilium tu quoque fontium,
> me dicente cavis impositam ilicem
> saxis, unde loquaces
> lymphae desiliunt tuae.

> O fount of Bandusia, brighter than
> crystal, worthy of sweet wine not with-
> out flowers, tomorrow you will be given
> a kid, whose brow just swollen with
> sprouting horns marks him for love and
> war; in vain: for he will dye your
> cold currents with his red blood, this
> offspring of a playful flock. The fierce
> season of the scorching Dog Star does not
> know how to touch you; you furnish de-
> lightful coolness to oxen wearied by the
> plowshare and to the wandering flock.
> You too will become one of the noble
> founts, while I sing the ilex imposed
> on the sloping stones whence leap your
> babbling waters.

Seeing that both animals represent elemental male
sexuality, the kid's sacrifice parallels that of the
boar in the Diana ode. But the effect upon us is profoundly different. Whereas the boar's blood seems intended to invigorate the phallic pine, the kid's is
soon dissipated in the fount's gelid swirl. Our
suboles is victim indeed. The image is the more
arresting in that a blood sacrifice to a spring is the
poet's invention. Wine and flowers (1. 2) were the
prescribed offering at the festival of the Fontinalia.
What, then, is Horace saying?

First, a few matter-of-fact observations. In form,
the poem is a hymn. Accordingly, the fount is a deity,
and as such, obviously, she is Horace's divine muse.

Also, she is virginal. If Horace does not say so explicitly, the combined qualities of crystalline purity
and unadulterable freshness place the issue beyond
doubt.[1]

The fount, then, is Horace's divine, virgin muse,
and as virgin, she is plainly inviolable. Thus, if the
imagery of blood cannot but suggest sexual initiation,
the evocation is ironic, the blood being the victim's
own. As muse, meanwhile, she is a fecund procreative
source. Far from contradicting this suggestion, on
mystic grounds, her virginity supports it. She is a
species of the Great Mother, ever prolific yet ever
virgin in her potential to create; and the kid is her
phallic victim. The central panel of Descende caelo
helps determine the rest. Its cohortis defessos parallels fessis tauris here, while the restorative virtue
of the frigus amabile answers to recreatis there. We
conclude that, like the muses of Pieria, the fount is
wholly alma. Let us not lose sight of the pathetic
phallic victim, however. For him the fount is wholly
devouring. Thus, Horace evokes the two proverbial faces
of woman, the dark goddess and the resplendent, with
rare, rich frugality.

We might also conclude that the case for the
transcendency of woman has rarely been more forcibly
put than in the Bandusia ode. Far from entertaining
such a thought, however, the poet proceeds to enact, in
the figure of the looming ilex that dominates the close,
as proud an assertion of the male principle as the Odes
contain.[2] Thus is the pathetic kid redeemed, and, all
in all, we could hardly have expected a different outcome.

205

Still, where the essential theme of poetic inspiration is concerned, the male principle plays a harmoniously cooperative role. _Frigus_ _amabile_ is the fount's boon to the world, but, as Horace frames the scene, this does not derive from the intrinsic freshness of its waters alone. The overarching ilex contributes its share. For is not shade too a _frigus_ _amabile_? And must it not help insure the fount's immunity to the midsummer sun? In short, the masculine ultimately combines with the feminine in purveying that _frigus_ _almum_ which renews not just flock and herd but, ever and again, the Horatian lyric.

From the shaded fount it is but a short step to the watered grove, anciently regarded as the haunts of the muses. They were regarded, that is, as places numinous with creative potency and hence with the force of inspiration. The Bandusia ode serves to show that exploitation of the sexual symbolism inherent in such a landscape will naturally heighten the impression of their creative powers. Thus we find the symbolic combination of tree and water in contexts that speak of inspiration as various as the Pindaric and the Callimachean.

At the beginning of _Descende_ _caelo_, Horace calls upon Calliope to sing a _longum_ _melos_--something Pindaric, in other words--and presently proclaims the muse's reaction (3:4, 6f.):

> Audire et videor pios
> errare per lucos, amoenae
> quos et aquae subeunt et aurae.

> I seem to hear you and to wander
> through sacred groves, beneath which
> delightful waters glide and breezes.

This seminal rush of inspiration is the more effectively imparted for being framed in the work's fundamental triad of sexual symbols.

Quem tu Melpomene (4:3) plays a slight variation upon the same theme. Not athletic or military success will make me glorious, vows the poet (10ff.),

> . . . sed quae Tibur aquae fertile praefluunt
> et spissae nemorum comae
>   fingunt Aeolio carmine nobilem.

> . . . but the waters which flow
> past fertile Tibur and the groves'
> dense tresses make me famous by virtue
> of Aeolian song.

Grove and stream, in other words, fashion (fingunt) his fame by fashioning his song.

With more complication and less magniloquence, the Pindar ode had visited the same symbolic scene just one selection previously (4:2, 27ff.):

> Ego apis Matinae
> more modoque

> grata carpentis thyma per laborem
> plurimum circa nemus uvidique
> Tiburis ripas operosa parvus
>   carmina fingo.

> In the manner and method of a
> Mantine bee toilsomely gathering

207

> pleasant thyme around the abundant
> groves and banks of watery Tibur,
> I, humble poet, fashion my laborious
> songs.

In the Latin, the imagery of gathering attaches alike to
bee and poet and so identifies the two all the more
closely. Equally so the reference to Matinus, a mountain close to Horace's birthplace. The poet thus
manages to stress not only the inconspicuousness of his
talent, but the humbleness of his origins--a major thematic grace in an ode which, for arch purposes, turns
throughout on the contrast between the large and the
small.

Pindarum quisquis studet is far and away the
lightest-spirited composition of the fourth book and,
Diffugere nives aside, its most successful. Though
none less than Fraenkel takes its subject to be politics,
that world merely furnishes its material. Its real
focus is poetic style, specifically, the contrast between Pindaric transport and Callimachean craftsmanship.
The one is large, the other small.

The object of the ode's fun is the addressee,
Antonius, an all but nameless poet who has been urging
Horace to compose an ode in the style of Pindar celebrating Augustus' exploits. It matters not that Horace
has already authored several works of the type.[3] He
disclaims all such talent and, with equal disingenuous-
ness, pronounces Antonius ideally suited to the task.

He starts the ode, however, with a dire warning
against any such undertaking:

208

    Pindarum quisquis studet aemulari,
    Iule, ceratis ope Daedala
    nititur pinnis vitreo daturus
        nomina ponto.

    Whoever strives to rival Pindar,
    Iulus, soars on Daedalean wings of wax,
    destined to give his name to a glassy
    sea.

The figure of winged ascent certainly suggests the
phallus, while, for the rest, Quis multa gracilis presents a sturdy parallel. Like Pyrrha's puer, a fledg-
ling in his own right, Pindar's unworthy rival is inadequate to his ambitions, and watery death is the
common doom. Immediately next, with a categorical impudence, our poet spins a period of twenty lines quite
in the manner of the Theban bard. Lest we miss his
purpose, he is most Pindaric at the start (4ff.):

        Monte decurrens velut amnis, imbres
        quem super notas aluere ripas,
        fervet immensusque ruit profundo
            Pindarus ore,

        laurea donandus Apollinari,
        seu per audaces nova dithyrambos
        verba devolvit numerisque fertur
            lege solutis . ₀ ₀

        Like a river streaming down a
        mountainside which rains have nourished
        till it has overflowed its wonted banks,
        Pindar seethes and rushes immeasurable
        with deep-throated roar whether he rolls
        out strange new words in bold dithyrambs
        and is borne on in measures freed of
        law . . .

Our main interest rests in the water imagery. First we
note the absolute change from <u>vitreo</u> <u>ponto</u> at the end
of the first stanza to the madly turbulent stream of
the Pindar simile. Waters, coming alive before our
eyes, are borne along in a rush that makes irresist-
able sense of the phrase <u>lege</u> <u>solutis</u>. Pindar's style
is in general like such waters, says Horace, but it is
not till we come to the mention of the dithyramb that
the inherent female symbolism attains its essential
point. The dithyramb was sung in honor of Dionysus,
whose votaries were women, whose rites were a manic
dance, "free of law." They dance in these lines.

Having thus linked Pindar's inspiration with the
feminine, the poet now proceeds to identify it with the
masculine, neatly revisiting the start in the process.
Both the stratagem's boldness and ingenuity keep the
Theban model well in mind (25ff.):

> Multa Dircaeum levat aura cycnum,
> tendit, Antoni, quotiens in altos
> nubium tractus . . .

> A great breeze lifts the Dircaean
> swan, Antonius, as often as he makes
> for the high cloudy tracts . . .

In the phrase <u>levat</u> <u>aura</u> <u>cycnum</u> we are presented with
three proven sexual images. If the indwelling sugges-
tion of phallic grandeur seems to comment not unpride-
fully on the bravura performance just enacted, Horace
hastens to erase the impression with the metaphor of
the Mantine bee which follows immediately. The upshot
is that, if he takes wing, it is only in the manner of
the humble bee. He is <u>parvus</u> (<u>l</u>. 31). Then Antonius

harvests a sudden and dubious reward (33f.):

> Concines maiore poeta plectro
> Caesarem . . .

> You, a poet endowed with a
> larger plectrum, will celebrate
> Caesar . . .

The plectrum was a simple stick and, in the undistinguished Antonius' hands, we may be sure, save for its phallic symbolism, only a stick. Horace has considerably more to say on the great and the small before the ode is finished, all of it hanging Antonius with a hollow grandeur. But the task is really completed in the thirty-third line.

One further reason why Horace strikes us as disingenuous in the Pindar ode is that he had come nicely to terms with the poetry of intoxicated rapture in two earlier odes to Bacchus. This is not to say that he does not remain wary of it. Where any form of emotional transport is concerned, his predilections are decidedly Apollonian. His attitude toward erotic passion is a fair case in point. It is dangerous, and he guards against it, for he knows that he cannot master it. But he also finds its wonder irresistible. So it is with Bacchic inspiration, and more so.

Amid a plethora of symbolism, the first of the two odes in question stresses the god's power (2:19):

> Bacchum in remotis carmina rupibus
> vidi docentem--credite posteri--
> Nymphasque discentis et auris
> capripedum Satyrorum acutas.

211

Euhoe, recenti mens trepidat metu
plenoque Bacchi pectore turbidum
    laetatur: Euhoe, parce Liber,
        parce gravi metuende thyrso!

Fas pervivaces est mihi Thyiadas
vinique fontem lactis et uberes
    cantare rivos atque truncis
        lapsa cavis iterare mella:

fas et beatae coniugis additum
stellis honorem tectaque Penthei
    disiecta non leni ruina
        Thracis et exitium Lycurgi.

Tu flectis amnis, tu mare barbarum,
tu separatis uvidus in iugis
    nodo coerces viperino
        Bistonidum sine fraude crinis:

tu, cum parentis regna per arduum
cohors Gigantum scanderet impia,
    Rhoetum retorsisti leonis
        unguibus horribilique mala;

quamquam choreis aptior et iocis
ludoque dictus non sat idoneus
    pugnae ferebaris: sed idem
        pacis eras mediusque belli.

Te videt insons Cerberus aureo
cornu decorum leniter atterens
    caudam et recedentis trilingui
        ore pedes tetigitque crura.

On remote rocks I saw Bacchus--
believe me, posterity--teaching atten-
tive nymphs and goat-footed satyrs,
their ears pricked to listen. Evoe,
my mind quakes with lingering fear, and,
my breast full of Bacchus, wildly rejoices: Evoe, spare me, Liber, spare
me, you who are dreaded for your mighty
thyrsus!

It is lawful for me to sing of
the tireless Thyades, the founts of
wine and the rich rivers of milk and
to tell of honey dripping from hollow-
ed trees. It is lawful too to sing of
the crown of your blessed consort set
among the stars, of the palace of
Pentheus shattered in grievous ruin
and of the destruction of Thracian
Lycurgus.

You bend rivers, you bend the
savage sea to your sway; drunk on distant peaks you bind unharmed the hair
of the Bistonian women with a knot of
vipers. When the impious cohort of
the Giants strove to mount to your
father's realms through the steep sky,
you turned back Rhoetus with the nails
and horrible jaws of a lion. Though
said to be more suited for dancing,
merriment and sport, yet you were
equally prominent in peace and war.

Cerberus, when he saw you resplendent with your golden horn, offered no
harm, but, brushing you lightly with
his tail, he touched your feet with his
triple tongue as you strode away.

The first four stanzas amount to an excursus on
the Greek concept of to deinon--the terrible-wonderful,
the awesome. The very opening vision, which we must
attribute to wine, but also to a touch of the thyrsus
(7f.), strikes the poet as wondrous and terrifying in
equal parts. For us it is crucial to understand that
the thyrsus, the emblem and instrument of Bacchus'
power, is consummately phallic. It is the miraculous
wand of life, wonderful for its creative powers, but to
be dreaded for its overbearing might.

Horace proceeds to enumerate its--which is to say, the god's--wonderful-terrible powers. First, his marvelous powers of fertility at line 10ff., where, through familiar imagery, the symbolism works both the female and male principles gracefully into a scene of miraculous generation; then, in the affairs of Pentheus and Lycurgus, his terrible powers of retribution.

After this, there remains no sign of resistance on Horace's part (the parce, parce of the second stanza), but only further testimony to the god's irresistible might. First he tells of the god's domination over the female. The power of his thyrsus over rivers and sea declare the theme in purely symbolic terms,[4] while allowing for the symbolism of separatis iugis, the remainder of the sixth stanza describes nothing so much as the god's sexual possession, as indolent as it is final, of his female votaries.[5] So far the stress has lain wholly upon the phallic might of the thyrsus, but, as Horace knew, Bacchus represented the ultimate androgyne. Hence there follows a subtle use of gestures affirming the female in nature.

At first glance, the image of the ravening lion is wholly male, but the emphasis upon the claws and, more especially, upon the devouring maw introduces a decidedly female note. For the effect we may compare 3:20, where Pyrrhus' rival for Nearchus' affections readies herself for his "swift arrows" by sharpening her dentes timendos. In either case, we have an adumbration of the dread vagina dentata.[6] Perceptibly, then, Bacchus has become female and male in one. Next, the poet disposes of the tradition that he is, in fact, more effeminate than virile by declaring him a compound of both natures.

Then the finale, reasserting the charmed stillness of the opening stanza, reconciles all. Its point, the god's power over death, though exquisitely dramatized by means of the fawning Cerberus, is fully captured only in the symbolism of the golden horn. "The horn," says Page, "is a very ancient symbol of strength, vigour, plenty and fertility." So too is the phallus, and the one symbol gives onto the other. The fact that this horn is golden--the tint of immortality--and gleams solitary in the nether shadows tells its own splendid tale.[7] Yet this is only half of what it tells. The horn is also the god's drinking vessel, a hollow purveying, in wine, the female life force at its most puissant. In the full symbolism of the golden horn, then, resides the god himself. Here is the integrated life principle and definitive triumph over death. Here too the nymph and satyr of the opening are reconciled anew, but now amidst a wonder that transcends joy and fear alike.

The second ode (3:25) stresses the power of the god's inspiration, which, consistent with the close of Bacchum in remotis, the poet accepts without trepidation. The ode begins in the full flood of ecstasy:

> Quo me, Bacche, rapis tui
>   plenum? Quae nemora aut quos agor in specus
> velox mente nova?

> Where, Bacchus, are you hurrying
> me, full of your spirit? Into what
> groves or caverns am I driven, fleet
> with new inspiration?

215

THE GOLDEN PLECTRUM

The conjunction of caverns, rather than waters, with the symbolic groves has its purpose, which surfaces immediately:

> Quibus
> antris egregii Caesaris audiar
>
> aeternum meditans decus
> stellis inserere et consilio Iovis?

> In what caves will I be heard
> devising to set the eternal glory
> of Caesar amidst the stars and the
> council of Jupiter.

Horace is clearly referring to Descende caelo, where, as we well know, the image of the Pierian cave dominates.

It will be a most original work, he continues, expanding upon the claim in a brilliantly imaginative passage (8ff.):

> Non secus in iugis
>
> exsomnis stupet Euhias,
> Hebrum prospiciens et nive candidam
> Thracen et pede barbaro
> lustratam Rhodopen, ut mihi devio
>
> ripas et vacuum nemus
> mirari libet.

> No differently does the sleepless
> Maenad gape from the heights as she
> contemplates the Hebrus and Thrace
> white with snow and Rhodope traversed
> by the feet of barbarians than I am
> charmed to marvel at banks and empty
> groves far from the pathways of men.

Those symbolic groves are as full of the symbolic powers
of inspiration as they are empty of rivals. But there
are perils too, save for the god's protection (14ff.):

> O Naiadum potens
> Baccharumque valentium
>   proceras manibus vertere fraxinos,
>
> nil parvum aut humili modo,
>   nil mortale loquar. Dulce periculum est
> O Lenaee, sequi deum
>   cingentem viridi tempora pampino.

>   O, potent over the Naiads and
> Bacchantes, who have strength to uproot
> tall ash trees with their hands, nothing
> small or humble of manner, nothing mortal
> will I sing. Sweet is the peril, O
> Lenaeus, to follow the god, binding my
> brows with the green sprays of the vine.

The devotion that can fortify our poet against the
perils implicit, especially on the symbolic level, in
proceras vertere fraxinos is without parallel in the
Odes. Still this is anything but idle prattle. The
high daring of Descende Caelo is what he has in mind.

Each of these pieces looks forward to the epilogue
of its respective book. With Bacchum in remotis the
epilogue ensues immediately. Hence, notice of the god's
immortality is followed by news of the poet's own, and,
more important, the symbolism of the refulgent horn is
succeeded by that of the soaring swan. Here, however,
all serious comparison must end. The epilogue to the
second book is a high flight of whimsy and little more.

Horace soberly informs Maecenas that he will never

217

die, that, simultaneously bard and bird, he will be
borne through "the liquid ether", leaving the earth
and its cities far behind. He attaches tangible evidence of the metamorphosis (9ff.):

> Iam iam residunt cruribus asperae
> pelles, et album mutor in alitem
> superne, nascunturque leves
> per digitos umerosque plumae.

> Even now rough skin settles in
> over my legs, while, above, I turn
> into a white bird, and smooth plumage
> sprouts on my fingers and shoulders.

Commentators and critics in herds have written off the
ode at this point. Many find the imagery aesthetically
repugnant, and even Fraenkel, who is singularly loathe
to disparage anything the poet undertakes, dismisses it
as "crude zoological precision."[8] But if we can accept
for a moment that Horace was aware of the crudeness,[9]
we are merely faced with the commonplace device of
deliberate bathos. Its purpose and effect is best seen
in the symbolism.

As a soaring swan, the poet appropriates all of
the phallic dignity that he later (4:2) ascribes to
Pindar by means of the same image and symbol, the very
dignity that he otherwise assigns to tree and horn in
passages that speak of poetic inspiration. All of this
he claims with perfectly exalted demeanor from the ode's
beginning to its end, save for the bathos just quoted.
Are his claims too exalted? The bathos suggests as
much. The passage, meanwhile, offers a distinction of
its own between the higher and the lower--the route that

bathos travels. <u>Superne</u>, there is snowy down; below,
the uncouth. So it is with the phallus perceived, on
the one hand, as the sacred talismen of renewal, the
golden bough, and, on the other, as the gnarled and
absurd virile appendage. The response, therefore, that
Horace descends from the sublime to the ridiculous in
one catastrophic step is well taken. Only he had hoped
to win a smile for it, the more charmed for its being
at his own cost. Unfortunately, he has sustained only
expense.

The case for phallicism is corroborated by the
second, more admired and altogether more earnest epilogue,
<u>Exegi monumentum</u> (3:30). Though this piece is several
odes removed from <u>Quo me Bacche</u>, the latter's <u>nil mortale</u>
<u>loquar</u> (<u>l</u>. 18) all but strikes its first chord:

> Exegi monumentum aere perennius
> regalique situ pyramidum altius,
> quod non imber edax, non Aquilo impotens
> possit diruere aut innumerabilis
> annorum series et fuga temporum.
> Non omnis moriar, multaque pars mei
> vitabit Libitinam: usque ego postera
> crescam laude recens, dum Capitolium
> scandet cum tacita virgine pontifex.
> Dicar, qua violens obstrepit Aufidus
> et qua pauper aquae Daunus agrestium
> regnavit populorum, ex humili potens
> princeps Aeolium carmen ad Italos
> deduxisse modos. Sume superbiam
> quaesitam meritis et mihi Delphica
> lauro cinge volens, Melpomene, comam.

> I have completed a monument more
> lasting than bronze and taller than the
> royal pile of the pyramids, which neither
> wasting rain nor mad Aquilo can destroy

> nor the immeasurable succession of
> years and the flight of time. I shall
> not die entirely, but a great part of
> me will escape the death goddess. I
> will grow, ever fresh with posterity's
> praise, for as long as the priest climbs
> the Capitol with the silent virgin. I
> will be famed where the violent Aufidus
> roars and where Daunus, poor in water,
> rules over a peasant folk, I, potent
> from lowly estate, the first to have
> adapted Aeolian song to Italian mea-
> sures. Accept the proud honor, Melpomene,
> gained by your merits and graciously
> crown my locks with Delphic laurel.

While the earlier epilogue turns on the conquest of
space, this announces the defeat of the inveterate
enemy, time. Both, however, figuratively stress the
ascendant strength of the phallus. Here the suggestion
first comes through in altius, is boldly resumed with
multaque pars mei and crescam and peeps through again
in ex humili potens. The part of Horace that will escape death is ostensibly his name, his reputation. That
he should invest this frail abstraction of the living
self with an archetypical symbol of thriving vitality
ought not to surprise, much less offend, anyone.[10]

Horace's finest tribute to the enduring power of
music concerns, however, not himself but Alcaeus. The
vehicle is Ille et nefasto (2:13), another ode which is
at best half understood outside of the symbolism. Even
its structure presents difficulties from the strictly
literal perspective. After an opening volley of curses
for a tottering tree which in its fall had nearly killed
him,[11] Horace closes the ode's first half with a sombre
excursus on the perils of chance.[12] Then remarking

that he had come terribly close to death, he proceeds to
a description of Sappho and Alcaeus charming the deni-
zens below, monsters and sinners included, with their
music.

Reversing an earlier consensus, Fraenkel states
unequivocally that the emphasis lies in the second half,
and few today would disagree.[13] But is the first half
then merely introductory? If so, why does it draw so
much attention to itself with its lurid burst of invective? How, moreover, does its sober philosophizing fit
in if, as Fraenkel states, the invective is offered in
a tone of light banter? How, above all, can half a
poem be accounted merely preliminary, especially in an
age that considered balance a categorical grace? Clearly, the business of the accursed tree would be better
off for a symmetrical correlative in the second half.

Let us get the relevant passages before us. First,
the curses:

> Ille et nefasto te posuit die
> quicumque primum, et sacrilega manu
>   produxit, arbos, in nepotum
>   perniciem opprobriumque pagi;
>
> illum et parentis crediderim sui
> fregisse cervicem et penetralia
>   sparsisse nocturno cruore
>   hospitis; ille venena Colcha
>
> et quidquid usquam concipitur nefas
> tractavit, agro qui statuit meo
>   te triste lignum, te caducum
>   in domini caput immerentis.
>
>
>   Whoever planted you, tree, both
> planted you on an evil day and reared

221

you with impious hand to be the destruction of posterity and a scandal
to the countryside. I could believe
that he broke his father's neck and
spattered his hearth with a guest's
gore in the dead of night. That man
has put his hand to the poisons of
Colchis and every villainy anywhere
conceived who placed you, dire tree,
in my field, destined to fall on its
unmeriting owner's head.

Now the scene in Hades (21ff.):

Quam paene furvae regna Proserpinae
et iudicantem vidimus Aeacum
    sedesque discriptas piorum et
        Aeoliis fidibus querentem

Sappho puellis de popularibus,
et te sonantem plenius aureo,
    Alcaee, plectro dura navis
        dura fugae mala, dura belli!

Utrumque sacro digna silentio
mirantur umbrae dicere; sed magis
    pugnas et exactos tyrranos
        densum umeris bibit aure vulgus.

Quid mirum, ubi illis carminibus stupens
demittit atras belua centiceps
    auris et intorti capillis
        Eumenidum recreantur angues?

Quin et Prometheus et Pelopis parens
dulci laborem decipitur sono,
    nec curat Orion leones
        aut timidos agitare lyncas.

How nearly I came to see the realms
of dark Proserpina, and Aeacus passing
judgment, and the seats of the blest set

apart, and Sappho complaining to the
Aeolian lyre of the townsgirls and
you, Alcaeus, intoning more amply with
your golden plectrum the rigors of the
sea, the rigors of exile and the rigors
of war! The shades marvel at both as
they sing words worthy of holy silence,
but, packed shoulder to shoulder, the
throng drinks in more eagerly tales of
battles and expelled tyrants. What
wonder if, amazed by these songs, the
hundred-headed monster lets its dark
ears droop and the snakes tangled in the
hairs of the Eumenides find rest? Why, even
Prometheus and Pelops' father are won
from their sufferings and Orion has no
care to chase lions or wary lynxes.

The antithetical emotions of the two passages--
rabid indignation giving way to a rapt tranquillity--
themselves go far toward solving the problem of unity.
Add that it is music which induces the change, and we
have the clue to the ode in every respect. I do not
refer merely to the music's power of enchantment in the
world below, but, more crucially, to its soothing effect
on Horace's own savage breast. Starting in hysterical
anger, he is, as it were, himself "won from his sufferings" by the very Alcaean lyre that he evokes.

Ingenious though this is, it is not till we fathom
the symbolism that we come into the ode's real tribute
to the power of music. Imagistically, the lignum
caducum dominates the first half, while the golden plectrum is the very cynosure of the second. Both phallic
emblems, their correspondence invests the ode with its
final shape and meaning. The tottering tree epitomizes
the fragile limits of manhood, the all too mortal condition. Here, ultimately, is the source of Horace's

philosophical mutterings, and hence too his curses.
But the golden plectrum shines imperishable amid the
final darkness.

Notes to Chapter One

1. M. Owen Lee, <u>Word, Sound and Image in the Odes of Horace</u> (Ann Arbor, 1969), p. 51.

2. Book IV appeared in 13 B.C., the primary edition in 23 B.C.

3. Achilles' failure to escape the rampaging Scamander by fastening onto a pine tree represents <u>in phallic terms</u> the pathetic antithesis to Odysseus' salvation by means of the fig. Among other sexual-symbolic touches in the <u>Odyssey</u> we may mention the description of Calypso's cave (5: 53ff.), the comparison of Nausicaa to a rising young (wherein lies the emphasis) palm (6: 162ff.), and the test of the bow (21: 117ff.).

4. "The Phantasies of Phaedra: A Psychoanalytic Reading," <u>The Classical World</u> (April-May, 1976), 435-442.

5. Jeffrey Henderson, <u>The Maculate Muse</u> (New Haven, 1974), p. 44ff.

6. Henderson, p. 48.

7. Henderson, p. 96.

8. For Lucretius, see Minadeo, <u>The Lyre of Science</u> (Detroit, 1969).

9. Thus, if I made no use of the evident sexual symbolism in the Archytas ode, the failure comes down to a poverty of imagination, not of method.

1. E. A. Fredricksmeyer, "Horace's Ode to Pyrrha,"
   Classical Philology (1965), 180-185.

2. Horace's invitation then, is not merely to drink.
   Recent scholarship has begun to see past suggestion of _skolion_ to the erotic interest beyond.
   See esp. R. G. M. Nisbet and Margaret Hubbard, _A
   commentary on Horace: Odes I_ (Oxford, 1970), p.
   135 and Hans Syndikus, _Die Lyrik des Horaz_ (Darm-
   stadt, 1972), p. 133.

3. The very meaning of his name, "master of festivi-
   ties," conduces to that conclusion.

4. The age (_veteres_) of the _orni_ and the funereal
   associations of the cypress help clinch the meaning.

5. Gilbert Murray, _The Classical Tradition in Poetry_
   (New York, 1957), p. 150.

6. Walter Wili, _Horaz_ (Basel, 1958), p. 182.

7. _Sinus_ suggesting either bosom and lap and _curvantis_
   reinforcing and supplementing the suggestion.

8. Time, he of course admits, saps the sexual powers,
   but that is a different matter. Neither the aged
   Lydia nor Chloris is impotent. Scarcely, meanwhile, does he suggest where the aged male is concerned that the continued pursuit of love is in-
   decent.

9. Cf. Steele Commager, _The Odes of Horace_ (New Haven,
   1962), p. 248 n.

10. Cf. C. B. Pascal, _Horatian chiaroscuro in Hommages
    a M. Renard_, 1, 622-637. Pascal well observes
    that the Quintilius piece serves as a bridge be-
    tween the Chloe and Lydia odes.

11. If Horace ends, as it seems, by accepting his own advice to the girl, "to pursue what is suitable to you (1. 29)"--thus aborting his erotic overtures-- it is the first hint in the <u>Odes</u> that the aging male might best look to the propriety of his sexual interests. It is clear, nonetheless, that the impropriety to which he admits consists more in a sense of inequality to the venture than anything else.

12. The meter of the two odes is also identical, the second Asclepiadean.

13. Each of the four Lydia odes thus shows a different shade of hostility.

14. See J. E. Cirlot, <u>A Dictionary of Symbols</u> (London, 1967), ad. loc.

15. Viktor Pöschl, <u>Horazische Lyrik</u> (Heidelburg, 1970), 180-196. What follows appeared in <u>Latomus</u> XXXIV (1975) 392-424 before I had become aware of Pöschl's essay. I am delighted to find that our findings correspond as closely as they do, but regretful that ignorance prevented due homage at the proper time.

16. It must be understood as well that by ancient norms domination over woman represents triumph over the Dionysiac in human nature, which is Horace's higher interest in this ode.

17. The phrase <u>summo carmine</u> contains even wider structural felicity in that this culminating song of Horace's last love song (a happy concinnity in its own right) concerns, as do the first and last love lyrics of the <u>Odes</u> itself, both love and death.

18. See esp. Edward Fraenkel, <u>Horace</u> (Oxford, 1966), 273ff.

1. For the latest such judgment see Nisbet and Hubbard, p. 59f. Curiously, though the authors deduce that Faunus in this stanza represents Priapus, they insist upon a "considerable slackening of tension."

2. The notice of mortality we gather from the word *Genuis* itself, for one's *Genius* is born and dies with the person.

3. Commager, p. 284.

4. The pun does not lie wholly in the phonetic similarity between *pinus* and *penis*, but in that similarity augmented by the symbolism of the huge pine.

5. A lesser affirmation comes with *lympha* etc., where the imagery, besides offering a female counterpart to the *pinus ingens*, suggests a struggle to remain vital, the struggle of life against death. Cf. Commager, ibid.

6. Commager, p. 285.

7. E. Zinn, Eranios, Festschrift für Hildebrecht Hommel (Tubigen, 1961), 185-212.

8. Pöschl, p. 236.

9. For a more colorful sexual-symbolic sketch of Tibur, see Prop. 3:16, 3f.

10. Commager, p. 277.

11. Commager, p. 280.

1. Kenneth Quinn, <u>Latin</u> <u>Explorations</u> (London, 1963),
   253ff. W. H. Friedrich, Nachrichten der Akademie
   der Wissenschaften in Gottingen, Philologisch-
   Historische Klasse 1959, 81-100, though he im-
   probably regards the relationship between Horace
   and Galatea as that between surrogate father and
   daughter, has seen deeply into the erotic nature
   of Europa's monologue.

2. Williams, p. 140. Friedrich, p. 91, goes so far
   as to postulate that Europa chose to cross the sea
   with the bull and even "entered into an agreement"
   with the creature.

3. Fraenkel, p. 193.

4. Friedrich, p. 92, justly points out the Ariadne-
   like tonalities of Europa's lament. We must
   strenuously resist the notion of a consummated
   love act, however. The sequence, rather, is
   closer to this: Europa was attracted to the
   bull, a datum of the myth, and so mounts him;
   once arrived in Crete, waking to the low, estrang-
   ing motive of her act, she reproaches herself for
   shamelessness; at the same time she unconsciously
   yearns for consummation and so inveighs not so
   much against the bull, but what she takes to be
   her abandonment.

5. Friedrich, p. 96, nicely observes that Venus' description of Europa's outburst characterizes nothing other than a lover's quarrel--another indi-
   cation that Europa protests too much.

6. See Fraenkel, 188ff.

7. "Horace <u>Carm</u>. 1. 14: What Kind of Ship?" <u>Classi-</u>
   <u>cal</u> <u>Philology</u>, LXI (April, 1966), 84-98.

8. Nisbet and Hubbard, ad loc.

9. It is worth recalling that in everyday Latin a ship _desiderata_ was a ship lost at sea.

10. Page, p. 441.

11. Fraenkel, 418 n.

12. E. A. Hahn, _Transactions of the American Philological Association_, LXXVI (1945), XXXII f.; N. E. Collinge, _The Structure of Horace's Odes_ (London, 1961), 75 n.; J. Perret, _Horace_ (New York, 1964), 179 f.; Quinn, 11 n.; Nisbet and Hubbard, p. 40.

13. In its own book, meanwhile, the grudging spirit of 4:12 is glaringly set off by the elaborate preparations for Maecenas' visit in the immediately preceding ode.

14. Cf. Fraenkel, p. 452.

15. Nisbet and Hubbard, ad loc.

16. It bears mention that we know of no voyage to Greece on Vergil's part save the ill-starred one of 19 B.C.

17. Syndikus, p. 59.

18. The attempt by Nisbet and Hubbard (ad loc.) to turn the insipidity to account only succeeds in boggling the imagination.

19. The case of Galatea is not really apposite. There Horace has obviously reconciled himself to the loss of the beloved. Here he has not.

20. See, e.g., J. P. Elder, _The American Journal of Philology_, 1952, 140-158.

21. At the same time, however, the expression (couched in commercial imagery) of misplaced trust at 11f. casts monitory shadows.

22. Page finds it a northerly, Bennett a westerly breeze, both on respectable grounds.

23. Chauncey Finch, "Fragments of a New Vita Vergiliana in Codex Reg. Lat. 1669," <u>The</u> <u>American</u> <u>Journal</u> <u>of</u> <u>Philology</u>, 1974, 56ff.

1. Commager, p. 240.

2. Commager, p. 263f.

3. For the sake of convenience I shall refer to the emperor by this title throughout.

4. This despite Fraenkel's finding to the contrary, p. 297.

5. The theme of secondness is cunningly exploited by a stanza (33ff.) which Fraenkel calls (p. 294), "one of the most bewildering passages in Horace's odes." The poet hesitates whether to name Romulus, Numa et al. second to (post hos) Hercules and the Dioscuri, whose mention closes the roll call of gods and heroes which had begun at line 13. When he later places Augustus second to Jupiter himself, the stupendous gap between the emperor and any previous Roman luminary comes subtly home to us.

6. Commager, p. 222.

7. On the architecture of the Roman Odes I follow Perret, who sees the first ode as introductory and the remaining five centering on Descende caelo.

8. Fraenkel, p. 267.

9. Pertinently, Commager observes (p. 227) that Plancus' consulship took place in 42 B.C., the year that Horace participated at Philippi.

10. This despite Fraenkel, p. 284f.

11. On the sublimeness of the poetic diction here, see F. Solmsen, "Horace's First Roman Ode," The American Journal of Philology, 58 (1947), 339.

12. The "shock" is of course alleviated in that the first two stanzas are as much an introduction to the ensemble as to the poem proper.

13. Williams astutely points out (p. 65) that, on the evidence of 33ff., the ancestral _delicta_ which Horace has in mind date from the close of the Punic Wars, 146 B.C.

14. Cf. Commager, p. 196, for the procreative implications of the imagery here.

15. Even the opposition is pointedly contrasted to Jupiter. It is _fidens_ (l. 50).

16. Cf. Williams, p. 128.

17. Fraenkel, p. 439.

18. Commager, p. 234.

19. So too in the lion's descent upon she-goats at 13ff.

20. At the same time, of course, the mythological association of rivers with bull-gods justifies his option.

21. Fraenkel's arguments to the contrary (p. 403ff.) lose sight of the distinction between the literal and the figurative in literary composition.

22. It is true that in 4:3 Horace attributes to Melpomene a fair share of the dignity that here goes to Apollo. That ode, however, is nothing like the reprise of _Descende caelo_ that this is. Most crucially, Melpomene is not the author of _lene consilium_ that Apollo is here.

23. Cf. Commager, p. 320.

24. Fraenkel, p. 426.

25. Commager, p. 321.

26. Though barely possible, it is irrelevant that the Lollius ode may have been written before his military disaster in 16 B.C. By the time of publication (13 B.C.), his name signified defeat.

Notes to Chapter Six

1. The fact that the virgin Neobule's soliloquy immediately precedes is also apposite.

2. For the strictly erotic implications of the closing stanza, see Chapter Two.

3. For Pindar's influence on Horace see Fraenkel, 283ff., 293, 426ff., 435.

4. It was the touch of Bacchus' thyrsus that parted the waters of river and sea in the course of his Oriental journeys.

5. I have translated the phrase "distant peaks," its traditional rendering, in order to secure literal sense. The primary meaning of _separatus_, however, is readily accomodated in the symbolism.

6. For the association of nails with female fury see 1:6, 18.

7. Cf. Mercury's _aurea virga_ (1:10, 18f.) for an allied but lesser effect.

8. Fraenkel, p. 301.

9. Cf. David West, _Reading Horace_ (Edinburgh, 1967), p. 91.

10. In this ode too an element of self-parodying clings to the symbolism, but, in the absence of anything outwardly ridiculous, it serves to relieve, rather than explode pomposity.

11. Strictly, Horace curses the tree's planter, but this is a clear case of deflection.

12. Horace's _improvisa leti vis_ doubtless derives from Lucretius' _vis abdita quaedam_ (5, 1233).

13. Fraenkel, p. 166f.

Index of Odes Cited

STUDIES IN CLASSICAL ANTIQUITY

Band 1:

Hoevels, Fritz Erik: Märchen und Magie in den Metamorphosen des Apuleius von
Madaura. Amsterdam 1979. 337 pp. ISBN: 90-6203-842-5   Hfl. 65,—

There are three discussions. In the first, the folk-tale motifs on which *Cupid and Psyche*
is allegedly based are traced to stone Age initiation rituals (in the manner of V.J. Propp),
to which Apuleius is in a sense regressing by redeploying the motifs in the cause of Isiac
religion. In the second, Freud reigns supreme: stone Age man, the inventress of *Cupid
and Psyche*, and Apuleius himself are shown to have suffered from repressed infantile
sexual curiosity — and Cupid stands in for the father in a female Oedipus-complex. In
the third, Africa and Apuleius become central to Late Antique Irrationalism.

Band 2:

Albert, Wolf-Dieter: Darstellungen des Eros in Unteritalien. Amsterdam 1979.
288 pp. ISBN: 90-6203-892-1   Hfl. 60,—

Ziel dieser Untersuchung ist, festzustellen, ob der Gott Eros in bildlichen Darstellungen
Unteritaliens in anderen mythischen und menschlichen Verbindingen auftritt als im
Mutterland, so dass daraus eine besondere und anders geartete religiöse sowie künster-
lische Erscheinung und Erfahrung für den Westen der griechischen welt erschlossen
werden kann.

Band 3:

Erickson, Keith V.: True and Sophistic Rhetoric. Amsterdam 1979. 427 pp.
ISBN: 90-6203-591-4   Hfl. 120,—

This book examines Plato's concept of true and sophistic rhetoric, the maturation of his
rhetorical theory, amatory persuasion, poetry, Isocratean rhetoric, Socratic chatter,
dialectic writing, and specific evidence of rhetorical theory in the 'Apology, Meno, Gor-
gias, Phaedrus, Symposium, Republic, Cratylus and Protagoras.' Overriding considerations were an article's general scholarship and interpretation of Plato. In addition, each
article was scrutinized for evidence of orginality, significance, relevance, and philological probity.